THE

Maine

STANDARD

Edited by Liza Gardner Walsh

Down East Books

Published by Down East Books

An imprint of Globe Pequot

Trade division of The Rowman & Littlefield Publishing Group, Inc.

4501 Forbes Blvd., Ste. 200

Lanham, MD 20706

www.rowman.com

www.downeastbooks.com

Distributed by NATIONAL BOOK NETWORK

British Library Cataloguing in Publication Information Available

Library of Congress Cataloging-in-Publication Data

ISBN 978-1-68475-114-3 (pbk.: alk. paper)

ISBN 978-1-68475-241-6 (e-book)

♾™The paper used in this publication meets the minimum requirements of American National Standard for Information Sciences—Permanence of Paper for Printed Library Materials, ANSI/NISO Z39.48-1992.

Contents

Winter Boat and Docks, by Hazel Mitchell

Obsessions
A Poetry Compilation

Introduction

The pages that follow are graced by the work of nine poets I had the honor and pleasure of facilitating a six-month course on the crafting of chapbooks offered through Maine Media Workshops and College in 2020. Though the course was entirely online because of the pandemic, it proved to be equally as powerful as in-person—perhaps more so—because it provided a much-needed, life-affirming space to create art despite the chaos engulfing the world
at the time.

Early in the course, I shared with them the notion that every poet is figuratively writing one poem all their life, meaning that a poet's body of work is informed by a unique obsession that has taken hold of them. As such, every poem is an attempt to investigate that obsession, to decipher some part of it, only to devise new questions about it, over and over again. Getting in touch with that obsession is key to finding one's voice and life's work as a poet.

These poets took that notion to heart and dove deeply and fearlessly into their obsessions. Their work expanded and flourished. What's more, in sharing their obsessions they bonded and became more intimate, insightful readers of each other's poems. They became obsessed with each other, so to speak. Two years since that course, they have continuously held monthly workshops together, resulting in these powerful, evocative poems before you. I congratulate them with humble gratitude for seeing all I wished for them to see in themselves, in their obsessions.

—Richard Blanco

John Paul Caponigro

Fishing

The sea only seems empty
because I am not in it,
ungilled, my body's no submarine, so
I plunge the lateral line of my emotions deep,
cast the nets of my mind wide, and
start dragging. Unsure,
what hook to bait, which line to use or
if it will break, but if not if
anything or nothing will come up and
no matter what I cast out,
what it will return to will not
be the same.

Rising

One sun in the sky,
a million stars upon the ocean.

Golden hours grow,
scorching eternity.

Ice loses its resolve
in uncountable drips and unstoppable drops.

Clouds make heavier descents;
winds multiply, coursing waves into new collisions.

Tides rise more, fall less,
even the great currents shift.

Mountains shrink from view, so
terrestrial becomes submarine.

Everything's moving into everything else.
Is this one great union or some abyss of chaos?

Memory's lost surface tempts us to
hope, *this was all a mirage.*

It's Raining Birds

It's raining birds. Nose-diving mid-flight, they're just falling out of the sky and hitting the ground. Their tiny songs are snapped from their necks and broken from their beaks. Flycatchers, swallows and warblers —no more. Reduced to feathers and bones with too little muscle and fat. They flew until they couldn't fly any more.

Rerouted from the tundra—from melting Alaska and defrosting Canada—diverted off the fertile coasts of Washington, Oregon, and California now full of fire, over the too-thin-to-live Chihuahuan

Desert, with too little touchdown and too little refueling, they never landed in their Central and South American wintering grounds. Grounded too soon, they became grounded permanently. Migration became starvation.

The evidence is just sitting here, piling up at our feet. Soon we won't be able to walk through all of our trespasses. One by one, drop by drop, in hundreds, in thousands, in hundreds of thousands, the sea of birds joins the ocean of the dead—three billion full in fifty years and counting . . .

Chrystena Hahn

Not the End

Poetry Master said,
There are many ways to die.

I did not die from the cancer;
I learned one way I might perish.
Atropos will determine
when and how
to cut the threads of my life.
When she arrives
I yearn to smile fearlessly,
to imagine driving on Belfast Road
autumnal trees—
verdigris and spruce,
orange, gold, vermilion—
cradling me,
to expect that, finally,

the hill that kisses the clouds
will have no other side,
will take me to the cosmos.

Parker's Piece
(for Stephen)

Absence of tending others' needs
leaves me brittle with the sensation
that I am the remainder
in a domestic subtraction problem.

Then, the cachet of your stint
teaching Wordsworth at Cambridge
pierces the notion that I am needed
at home, residual. You ask me to come.

Skittish traveling alone, I endure
the long night's journey to London,
the bus through hamlets, long highways,
to arrive at Parker's Piece.

You find me walking to the flat
on Midsummer Green. In your smile
I know again the breathless early years.
You want to inhabit this space together. I soften.

Climbing the steps to the second floor,
excited as a new bride, we inspect the rooms together,
then cross the green where community cattle graze
to a pub on the River Cam.

Exhausted, we return and go to bed.
I listen as you tell me about the owls—
especially the one whose whoosh and deep hoot
leads the parliament.

The cool of night overcomes.
Nestled into you,
I sleep the sleep of one protected,
learn again to be your wife.

Trip to the Underworld

Dreaming, I become Virgil,
can cross to the other side
of the roiling river.
My long-dead father
tells me to go find my mother,
but when I get to her,
she looks at me in horror:
Get back! she commands.
Lethe has not let her forget.

My mother lived
much of her life in fear of loss.
When we were young, she'd pull
my sisters and me close
as she sat away from windows
during thunderstorms,
troubled even as the tempest
had just begun to brew.
If my father were late from work
She would stand at the window

wearing the harrowed look of a widow
till she heard his car pull up.
This intensified as she grew old.
When it rained hard, she feared inundation.
If it snowed, she pushed the storm door
back and forth creating something of a path
so sure she was of being trapped.

I have missed her since her death.
I never could shield her
as she protected me.
Still, I am relieved she is gone
and does not live in this world
where fear of loss paralyzes love.

Christine Terp Madsen

Tall Pines

Spires pierce the sky,
Taller than the cathedral,
Taller than the jets can fly,
Or so it seemed.

Clouds pierce the sky,
And send puffs of smoke
To the silent ground
Or so it seemed.

Bluets pierce the ground
Small bursts of blue and white

With a ring of gold
Or so it seemed.

Hidden birds pierce the air
Their calls a mystery
To all who listen
Or so it seemed.

I stood among the pines,
Alone with them, the bluets,
The clouds, the birds,
Or so it seemed.

Fifty years have passed
Since I stood there.
They must still exist
Or so it seems.

To My Sister About Her Daughter

At the birth of your first child
Your face changed before my eyes.
Before you held your daughter,
you saw oceans of possibility in her eyes,
the world in the light beyond the stars.
Your blood races through her.

We are all mostly memory with a bit of blood thrown in.

When you were three years old and I was five we rode a float in the sea,
my hair in pigtails yours in blond ringlets, giggling in the waves
at Aunt Rik's on Long Island—I can remember her laughing.
When your daughter was three her hair in blond ringlets

she threw herself at me in the shallow ocean waves,
daring me to catch her—I caught my breath first, thinking she was you.

We are all mostly memory with a bit of blood thrown in.

Memory moves us from one day to the next,
keeps our feet moving forward, our minds looking backward,
our hands clasped together.

You move with authority across the tennis courts,
all legs and arms in six different directions,
your shots as sure as the next ocean wave.
Jen ran to catch you, pirouetting between points.
She combined her repertoire into a fluid, unstoppable motion
When she shone as a lacrosse player.

We are all mostly memory with a bit of blood thrown in.

Detritus Floats

Jetsam is a shortening of jettison
There is no shortening of moving.
It is all work, from start to finish.
You have to attach buoys to everything,
Make them ligan,, to find them again after the move.

The boxes multiply, the bubble wrap consumes,
the newspaper, once a dread to recycle, grows scarce,
and detritus floats. (Not from rocks, but from life.)
Spiral notebooks and unspiralled tape measures,
paper clips and nail clippers. It clogs the air
swimming in lazy circles around my eyes.

It can't be boxes, it can't be gathered.
It is amorphous, it is spiritless.
It is loose buttons and loose change,
forgotten greeting cards and last year's calendar.
I focus on your card, you who I no longer love,
and will it from my sight. It falls into the abyss.

Shawne McCord

A Swelling Mass

I feel a wet tear,
perched
on my bottom eyelid,
cradling the ache:
a branch, wildly ripped off
my sturdy trunk,
whose open
wound is no longer
raw and exposed,
but lightly weathered,
soft and gray.
A swelling mass
on the verge of falling.
But no,
I blink three times.
Disperse,
dissipate,
dissolve.
And the ache?

Like the living
blind roots burrowing below,
seeking sustenance from
composted,
compacted,
composed
earthy matter,
it twists, in a slow,
unpredictable dance,
as it edges toward
a once embolden boulder
that rumbled with
mammoth ice bergs,
now together
encapsulated
enclosed,
encased
in rich matter.

A buried ache,
surfacing, again,
a droplet swelling
on my eyelid.

Summer Summons

I.
Go, turn over the leaf,
Uncover breath and earthworms,
Inhale levity, exhale.

II.
Stretch arms toward the rain,
Let droplets meet facial freckles,
Soak up random gifts.

III.
Curve slightly, as feather
Do si dos down, before toes.
Possibilities.

IV.
Dance like flames ignite,
Sizzling scenarios,
Emanating warmth.

V.
Go, turn over a leaf,
Uncover breath and earthworms,
Inhale, exhale.

Letter to my First Daughter

You entered this world when the moon
was a sliver. A simple sliver, bright on an August night.
No birth is simple though, so let's leave simplicity to the moon.

Take a woman, your mother, me, in a mental stew of studies, juggling
childhood
philosophy, theory, and technique with ease. Take this same woman,
your mother, me,
with no knowledge of how to love a brand new baby.

Now, add a midwife, my expert other, to my bulbous side, as I waddle
around and around a sports field. Now add your faithful father,
nervously navigating the highway to the hospital, as my guttural moans
penetrated his concentration. As the doors slide open, I am instructed to
lie on the stretcher (because that's the law). This caused electrical shocks
to reverberate through me, all of me. So I refused this law and order.
Pain could be avoided if you,
beautifully big in my belly, could hang down.
So I, hands and knees on top a sterile stretcher, was rolled while high
off the ground,
to the room, with a narrow window, where you, with a little help from
my body's uncontrollable, unpredictable hurtful heaving, you, in your
time, through searing sensations
that I wouldn't avoid, slid, screaming into this world,
my world, now our world. That's when the moon sliver shone on you.

Have you ever, maybe in a dream, entered a very important gathering
of melodic conversation and laughter, and realized everyone is speaking
in words you don't understand?
You're supposed to be happily engaged, but you feel lost?
You, dear one, with auburn curls, and feisty swirls, stiff stance, caring
glance, you made your points and you stood your ground.
I had to learn how to hold you, with no time for research,
swing you, with no time for theory,
love you, no, really love you,
under the ever changing moon,
my mighty one.
I'm still learning.

Audre Minutolo-Le

Doing Laundry Near Selfoss

The sky was falling.
Yes, the sky *does* fall and I could see
the gray in the distance, threatening
sheets of rain coming closer, that cold
summer day in the Icelandic North.

My linens and intimates spread
out on teak chairs and tables, whipping
in the wind, begging for attention.
The laundry rack, with its loose rod,
barely held itself together, crying for help.

All of those sheets and panties and cases
frenetic in their quest to dry, to beat the weather,
for the dryer had shunned them, not answering
their wetness, except for a tumble.
Tumble. Stop. One way, then the other.

Once, along the Roman Road in Wilmington,
South Downs Way in the distance,
I did laundry in the English summer sun, my twin
daughters' same-but-different shirts and skirts
clipped to the line, baking in the heat of the still Sussex air.

Long Man watched over, his shape outlined in chalk
against the grassy hill. A black sheep darted along the footpath.
Cows witnessed from behind the stiles
as I pulled the small clothes off the line, stiff and dry,
and tossed them into the wicker basket.

And once at a hostel in Puerto Madryn, our clean laundry
hung limp, drying in the South American sun.
Do you remember? It was the morning after the night
I went alone to watch the writhing Tango dancers at the local bar —
the year you finally made an honest woman of me.

That morning I couldn't help but notice the blond
American girl who lay face down on her towel
in the grass, fenced-in by the yard. She cried softly,
ashamed because she had slept with the boy from Ireland.
Or was it the boy from England? Those young men in their shorts,

bare-chested, leaned back in their chairs in the hot open game room
drinking Mate, their minds filthy with travel, staring across the lawn
at her in blame, as if she needed a good hosing
down. In a crying heap, she lay alone waiting
like dirty laundry being hung out to dry.

The Guinea Pig
¡Buen provecho!

Remember that night in Buenos Aires?
No, it was Cusco, Peru.
Yes, there, on the old Inca trail
where the Machu Picchu stones
were laid four square home

and the drunken man lay in the gutter.
You lifted him off the cobblestone
sidewalk to save him —you, a savior —
so that he wouldn't die
while Peugeots and Fiats whizzed by.

Later, we walked on the well-worn streets,
slab on slab of puzzle-pieced stones,
worshipping the deities.
At Paddy O'Flahrety's in Old Cusco
the young couple spoke in Germanic mews

and the English bloke shouted out clues
to the expats playing Trivial games
in pursuit of happiness at the bar.
Your anger simmered low then
the python struck sharp and hard.

For dinner, you ordered *Cuy* and the waiter
placed before me a sizzling dish
dark and pungent. A hot breeze spun
a delicate softness over her blackened skin.
She had become the main dish.

Still smoldering, her cooked flesh
slumped over a fragrant bed of rice.
Her tiny legs, ears, and gnawing little teeth
dark brown from the South American heat.
Perhaps she felt useful again, if not
burnt to a crisp.

September Evening, 1917

What is this hand-knotted beige and rose wool rug
and Edison's graphophone wax-cylinder song
playing on the warm summer porch as the gliding sofa
sways back and forth, back and forth?

What do Edison's graphophone song on the Home model

and Edna St. Vincent Millay's *Renascence* have to do
with this married couple's late-summer porch evening
and wind whistling through the windows as waves roll in?

The sunset has left the Camden Hills black
on their late-summer porch looking out at the Bay.
He asks her to slow down as they sway back and forth on the glider
and she scoffs as they settle into the truth of marriage, husband and wife.

The pace is not right, she says. The needle scrapes
"You Are My Sunshine," wax cylinder song spinning, waves rolling in,
hand-knotted beige and pink rose wool rug witness
to the late summer evening graphophone song of love.

White lace curtains billowing in the breeze
Soft waves rolling in, "You Are My Sunshine"
playing on the graphophone as they sway
back and forth in the depth of marriage — and leaving.

Soon he will leave this place of Home and the depth of marriage
and the gliding metal sofa will remain.
A long marriage, though they haven't yet found a rhythm.
The pace is not right, she says again.

And the graphophone stops.

Pam Burr Smith

Intoxicating Hope

I was once part of a trivia team
called Poor Dead Rhonda.

We played Wednesday nights at an Irish Pub
down by the train tracks.
I drank ginger ale during these bouts
believing temperance would beckon memory.

Most of the time, we came in second, or fourth.
The team that always won was a bunch of librarians
and high school teachers.
They should have been in another league,
or taken a few Wednesdays off.
But they loved crushing the rest of us
week in and week out.

Poor Dead Rhonda soldiered on in that dimly lit room
in the delicious hope that one night, just one night,
the stars would align in a sublime pattern,
and we would win.

Late Afternoon, Logan Airport, 2019

He sits one empty plastic seat away from me
in a crowded corner of the airport hallway
and he starts to sing a love song

in English, in a beautiful, trained, unselfconscious tenor
at perfect volume. Aimed it seems, at me and
everyone else. Full, round, lovely and wanted,

his voice goes through us.
When the song is over its absence resounds.

I wonder if I'm brave enough to talk to him,

as, eyes closed, he leans back and catches his breath.

The other people in the room are busy pretending
nothing just happened. As though gorgeous opera
occurs everyday in this gritty corridor.

And I know I have to, so, normal voice, conversational,
I ask, *Do you often sing in places like this?*

He turns himself toward me, and says softly, *Only
when somebody nearby talks loudly on a cell phone.*

It was such a heart filled song,
I know there's more to it than that, and then he adds,
My wife died last year, and I'm off to see the grandkids.

I look at the slumped nylon bags all over the floor,
and the people punching fingers at hand held devices.

Out the window, sleek silver planes wait in frigid air
for the rush of feet, the stumble of travelers who are
somewhere between here and where they plan to be,
with no time to notice the small miracle beside us.

Foggy Afternoon Walk

A large number of ducks were involved
in a walking migration,
from the creek they inhabit on Richard's Drive,
to the front yard of the gray house
near the meadow. At least a hundred of them,
a congregation moving in smallish clumps,

cacophonous and graceful,
dared the misty road, and sidled or trotted across.

Every time a car appeared through the fog
arrangements were improvised. Negotiations
varied with each encounter. Sometimes, the car
stopped and the ducks continued, silent
through wavering headlight beams.
Other times, the ducks retreated to the shadows,
squawking their disgust.

In the end, a reckless car came. Driving fast.
It swerved toward eight or ten ducks
spotlighting their feathered, vulnerable majesty
in the middle of the glistening road.
I screamed from the sidewalk,
covered my face with my arms.
And the ducks flew away.
I had forgotten they had wings.

Susan Tenney

Polka-Dots

Polka-dots...
Polka-dots are often found on things for children.
Why do you think that is?
Is there something benevolent about
little round colorful spheres?
Playfully scattered—other times in orderly patterns
dancing cheerfully on fabrics, clothing and curtains—
prancing on plates, cups or bowls—

Whether worn or not worn they do affect.
I know the polka-dot may at first appear of little import,
inconsequential, a meaningless little orb.
Sometimes clowns are costumed in polka-dots
yet I don't think they are inherently funny.

With all the injustices that flood our world,
the violence and slaughter of the innocents,
the destruction of our planet, with our lack of regard for nature,
when deep in damp tunnels of darkness my
mind cannot arrest these thoughts—I crawl under the polka dots.

Hard to breathe with all that is hurled upon us
under us, in front of us, around us
the constant thundering divisiveness seems never ending.
Sleep becomes up and up becomes exhaustion
Alone searches for community,
communities can terrify...

The simple blessing of the bee, the towering infernos of Monsanto
The color of people's skin and how that is a *thing* for humans
Dogs don't discriminate with differently colored dogs
Tropical fish swim side by side
The polka-dots of my crisp duvet cover, shower me with a rainbow of
          colors
and I am that child again.

I would live in a colorless world if
that is what it would take for us all to live as one—breath
Goodbye dear yellow of buttercups, goodbye cerulean, goodbye, goodbye
          sweet
sandberry red—the world is but a little sphere in

this vast universe of stars, planets, patterns of patterns, among patterns
       of points.
Just a polka from crib to death, from speck to the infinite
a single sphere, that could be
a polka-dot.

The Purchase

It was a lone bowl
of Italian design
kilned in China
purchased at the discount store
because
the colors were
fresh
generous and
optimistic:
qualities missing
in my single-parent life.
Rose-orange
of a blushing sunset
belonging to an early evening wish
for a conversation with a new friend.
A sweeping blue
the color of the Adriatic
brushed with beckoning currents I
wanted to be enveloped by
and
a green
like summer grapes
partnered
with a sunny yellow:

a promise of a bright day
right in the center
where the spoon
dips in.

The Roses

Beloved,
Your love, your spontaneity, out in search of a metaphor, in early hours of
this ordinary Saturday
returning with oranges and roses spread over the kitchen counter to greet
my ten o'clock eyes.
You are my Petit Prince.
But, loosening their cellophane negligees, their leaves fell off.
All of them
plunk, plunked plunk plunk,
like rain drops down
All but
the red
closed buds,
stuck on the ends of long stripped stems.
Looking like guilty greyhounds, embarrassed, wanting to slink away.
Silly and anemic.
Undressed but not sexy.
Sad. Naked.
Ridiculous in the vase.
Your gift
ruined.
So,
I complained about the roses
I did
I complained about the roses—I complained about all twenty-four.

Jumped in the car, hair uncombed
night shirt and sweatpants
Stormed in to Whole Foods, walked right up to the Flower Man
and said:

My Love, spontaneously this morning, for the Love of his life...

Flower Man:
Strange. I've never heard of such a thing- all the leaves falling off the roses...
No, I'll have to speak to my District Manager.
Our roses come from Columbia Ma'am, who knows what they do to them
there.
You have no receipt, Ma'am
Yes, I know...and because you have no receipt
We cannot give you store credit.

Oh plunk, plunked plunk plunk...

Beloved:
Jellybean...It's unexplainable...ssshhh just...unexplainable
like love
itself.

Meg Weston

For the Volcano Pilgrim

Poet Disappears on a Volcano
Craig Arnold's blog: *Volcano Pilgrim*
the island: *Kuchino-erabu, Japan*

A seeker
of words
his footprints
going up
the path
no sign
of return
last entry:
Angelica
Ashitaba
tomorrow leaf
in Japanese
it's said
to give
long life
to Izu islanders
but not to this poet.

I drank water
from a bucket
at a Japanese
shrine where
you may choose
to drink from
only two
of three
buckets:
long life,
happiness
or wisdom.
Perhaps he
chose the
latter two.

I write
for a pilgrim
of poetry
who loved
the mountains
and the fire.
I hear his verse
in the throb
of the earth's
heart pulsing;
in deep time's rhythm
sounding like
freight train
reverberating
in the ground.

I see the sun
rise red over Japan
the clouds
reflecting lava
gushing skyward
the stars
glittering overhead,
angelica
growing wild
on tangled slopes—
steam rises,
blurs the image,
and he is gone.

Did You Know that Volcanoes Sing Before They blow?

My phone ringtone is Jimmy Buffet. *I don't know,*
I don't know where I'm a gonna go
when the volcano blows...
I turn the phone ringer to silence.

Listening to the sounds of the earth might save your life....
I listen for the physics of earth's music—liquid pools
of magma beneath the crust playing tones
like water glasses filled to different levels.
I've listened to the breath of volcanoes before:

Etna's heavy breathing, slow and rhythmic,
that time I climbed past danger signs
up towards the crater, stopping short
of the edge, to listen.
The next day another man's footsteps
leading to the edge but not returning.

I've listened to Kilauea in the morning,
restless, crackling, whispering bubbles
of pahoehoe flows in Halemaumau's crater
just before dawn, light seeping over the horizon.

I didn't listen when my phone rang one afternoon.
I switched it off to continue my nap
thinking I'd call my brother later. No one
answered, so he drove himself to the hospital while
having a stroke. Foolish I'd say later, but luckily,

it wasn't too serious. Just enough
that we now answer each other's calls

holding our breath until the other says,
nothing's wrong, just checking in...

I think of the warnings the earth gives
of magma's movements, rising to the surface,
harbingers of destructions, no one knows
the exact timing of an eruption, all we know
is to answer the phone while we are still alive.

Stromboli

I remember getting off the ferry,
the island of Stromboli,
the last stop of the day,
the black silhouette of the volcano,
rising above white-washed houses
on the slopes under a blue sky.

I remember the crowds buzzing
around me in a language I didn't know,
unloading our luggage, helping
our film crew with mountains of gear,
stacking it on the pier, and the boat
turned around to head back to Milazzo.

The next day the Travel Channel would film us,
after climbing the mountain, you, just fifteen,
scrambling ahead of me, hiking up
your baggy pants that looked as if
they might fall to your knees,
you would read the volcano rap song

you wrote, while the fireworks of eruption
filled the evening sky behind you.

I remember looking for you when we were still
on the pier, realizing you didn't get off the boat,
knowing you had fallen asleep —
you always slept deeply — and trying
to make myself understood at the ticket
office where they spoke no English,
finally rocking my arms saying Bambino
and pointing to the rapidly disappearing boat.

I remember the boat turned around,
and you had made friends with all the crew,
who were waving goodbye when you
were returned to me, and we promised
that neither of us would tell your father,
my brother, although we both did.
I remember twenty years later you called me
and said you would call every day if I wanted,
and I said, no, once a week is enough,
if you promise to call.
The next day you injected Fentanyl
into your arm and eclipsed into sleep.

You kept your promise that first week,
returning in my dream, telling me you
remembered to call. But you haven't come
back again, and now all I can remember
are all the times I had failed you and left
you aboard the boat.

Lucinda Ziesing

She's Gone

The fire in Four Mile Canyon
scored the hillsides.
Then it rained for eight days.
The mountain fell down around her ankles.

She's gone.
Salina Junction swiped clean.
Our cabin on the creek, swept away.
Splinters of her floating in Boulder Creek.

She wasn't much to look at,
a dusty green asphalt shack.
You'd kick back the screen door on the way in
to stop the slam.

Inside, a temple of sound.
Our bedroom's a listening room
with windows hinged open to the creek.
A music box, whose lid never shuts.

My boyfriend, Wyck, panels her
in burnt-honey boards
with shelves for our books and LPs.
Bob Dylan's *Nashville Skyline* plays;
Lay lady lay, lay across my big brass bed.
Macramé hung philodendrons
thrive in the canyon's low light,
as do I.

Crystals in the windows
send tiny rainbows across our walls.
Vietnam is raging.
I tack a white piano shawl
embroidered in pink roses to the ceiling.
It pillows over us.
The breeze stirs the fringe.
The creek rushes through me.
Wyck's body pulls me
to planets beyond my solar system.
Charismatic and mercurial.
His humor breaks me in half.
Eyes the color of forget-me-nots;
blue with a dot of yellow at the stem.
I think our love can stop a war.
That was before he found cocaine.

After years of being told not to have desire;
it's only for bad girls.
I want it all now.
By winter
ice came and the snow was up his nose.
Even the Dalkon Shield doesn't protect me.

The geese migrate without me.
I don't hear them call
as they fly overhead.
On the cold bathroom floor
alone that night
miscarrying blood and the baby.

I left the Junction before winter could.
Never to sit naked in the creek

in the heat of summer again.
Never will…
she's gone.

The Library

The Library is Daddy's den.
Inside stone blue walls
where fires smolder at the edge
and winds blow cold over the sea.

My mother tells me to go there
when I'm just home from school.
I dread the walk to the far end of the house,
over a Persian rug plateau,
through a valley of chintz and Chippendale.
With no lights on there's plenty to break.

I cross a black and white linoleum bridge
into a sunroom.
His door's ajar,
a bitey smell of pipe tobacco.
I hear the fire pop,
the swill of ice in a glass.

The plate glass window
becomes a mirror.
The cardinals are missing from the feeder.
I watch a wind stir up in him.
He paces the room
lurching from his own darkened sky.
 "What have you ever done in your life to please me?"

The revving of an engine
that could run me over.

He places the yellow pad
and a sharpened pencil on the card table.
Then there's the math problem:
"A cabin cruiser left the harbor,
traveled to a small island at 24 mph.
On the return it traveled at 16 mph.
The total time of the trip was 5 hours.
How far was the island from the harbor?"
I have no idea.
I always get lost at sea.

Homage (an ekphrastic poem)

The H is silent
in Homage.

When you say it
the jaw drops.
A sound laments
from your gut, "aa-mage."

You're an honor guard.
Your lace drapes
over the remains.

You remember
when every town in America
had its Elm Street.
You stood watching

the parade under a shelter
flush with pride.

That was after the great planting
when streets were lined
with the American Elm.
Magnificent fluted vases
of leafy limbs allowing sun
to speckle the ground.
Like ballerinas, they beckon you
into a republic of shade.

In a blue pram
my mother's pushing me
on rolling white wheels.
Einstein walks by us
on his way home
under the elms.
She whispers,
"His head's down.
What we did to Japan
haunts him."

That was in the early 50's
When they declared an end
to the age of the great Elm.
77 million dead from a fungus,
brought from Europe in logs
to make furniture.
There's no cure
once a tree's infected.

They were never meant
to be planted
so close together in rows.
Only loosely
around a farmhouse.

Reckless for enchantment.
They call it human error.
The H is not silent in Human.

Homage.
When you say it
a sound laments
from your gut, "aa-mage"

A western shawl drops
down her back.
Halyna Hutchins,
Ukrainian Cinematographer,
shot by a prop gun on set
at the Bonanza Creek Ranch.
The feeling in her legs is gone.
She floats off her saddle
across the vermillion desert
becoming the texture and light
of her brilliant mind.
The cinematic moment
of her death rolling.

It was an accident, they say
losing life making art.
Negligence put a bullet in
where blanks belonged.

The H is not silent.

Hollywood lights candles
for their fallen rising star.
You sink to your knees.
You too leave the candle burning
inside a glass jar.
You cover the remains
with lace.
You pay Homage.

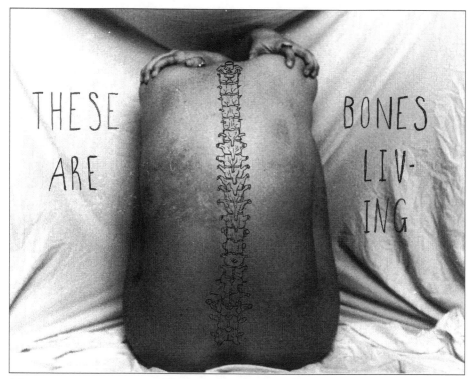

These Bones Are Living, a photo series by Phoebe Walsh

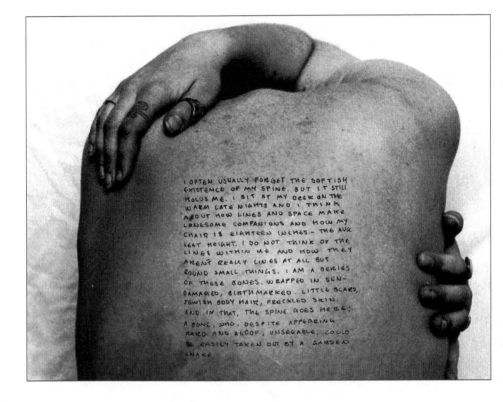

I OFTEN USUALLY FORGET THE SOFTISH
EXISTENCE OF MY SPINE, BUT IT STILL
HOLDS ME. I SIT AT MY DESK ON THE
WARM LATE NIGHTS AND I THINK
ABOUT HOW LINES AND SPACE MAKE
LONESOME COMPANIONS AND HOW MY
CHAIR IS EIGHTEEN INCHES — THE AVG
SEAT HEIGHT. I DO NOT THINK OF THE
LINES WITHIN ME AND HOW THEY
AREN'T REALLY LINES AT ALL BUT
ROUND SMALL THINGS. I AM A SERIES
OF THESE BONES. WRAPPED IN SUN-
DAMAGED, BIRTHMARKED. LITTLE SCARS,
JEWISH BODY HAIR, FRECKLED SKIN.
AND IN THAT, THE SPINE GOES HERE:
A BONE, WHO, DESPITE APPEARING
HARD AND ALOOF, UNSEEABLE, COULD
BE EASILY TAKEN OUT BY A GARDEN
SNAKE

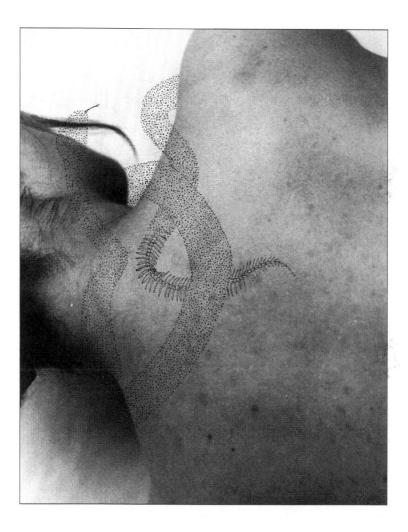

Fish, Birds, Light
Laura Bonazzoli

Impermanence.

It's what they tried to teach us at the monastery.

Of course it was the most important lesson. At the time, though, long before we met, I resisted.

On my board, I painted fish. Koi. Orange and pink and turquoise and black with little hills of blue.

Everyone said, How beautiful! Fish swimming in a pond of blue sand.

The final morning, the monks made me sweep it into the stream.

They wouldn't even let me take a picture.

Nothing, they said.

All gone.

And smiled.

And I let it go.

I should have learned the lesson then. Or practiced until I did. Instead of herbs—echinacea, yarrow—I should have planted daylilies. Instead of lamps, lit candles. Instead of love letters, written the word *fugacious* ten thousand times, then burned the paper.

It might have helped.

Yesterday, for instance. When I saw your parents' letter, your father's handwriting, and for one crazy second thought it was from you.

Or any day these last three years.

Pick one.

Pick today, for instance.

This morning, for instance, when I went down to the pond to fill my watering can and heard the little slapping sound and followed it— curious, but not in any hurry—just in time to see a silvery minnow flip-flopping its danse macabre, its scales sparkling with reflected light. I knelt, reached out my hands and scooped it up, wanting to give it back to the pond. But it was already limp, its eyes blank.

How did it come to be there? Perhaps a gull had dropped it. Who knows why anybody, anything, comes to be anywhere?

Frayed wire, for instance. Cellulose insulation, for instance. An argument, topic unrecalled. A young man, a father, knocked out on Ambien, alone in bed. A young woman, a mother, sleeping down the hall with her son.

I tried to wake you, Ren.

I swear I tried.

I know. Let's not start that again. If we do, I might have to accuse you of sending that poor little fish just to make me watch it suffocate to death.

Did you?

Send it to me?

Because if you did, I suppose I should at least be grateful that you chose a school day so I was spared having to hide my snorty little sobs from our son.

He thinks you're dead, you know. By which I mean he thinks you're gone permanently. And of course you are. To him.

Aren't you?

You don't haunt him, too, do you?

Because if you do, Ren, I swear I'll kill you. Someone around here—maybe that Catholic priest who's always out walking alone, or someone from that Spiritualist group on the coast—somebody should be able to perform an exorcism. Though I suppose the Spiritualists don't want to get rid of ghosts. They want to make contact. At least, that's what Pauline used to say. The woman who worked at the post office, I mean. The talkative one who always seemed so happy when I came in early in the morning before the mail was out and there weren't any other customers and she could just talk and talk and I couldn't ask her to shut up. She seemed to consider it her duty to fill me in on all the town gossip.

But not normal gossip, like most people tell. Strange things. Like she asked me once if I ever wondered about the house with all the dolls staring out the front windows. I sort of shrugged and nodded, and she said it belonged to an old gentleman—Leopold Siefert—whose wife died young of some sort of rare genetic disease, and there were two children, a boy and a girl, and the girl inherited the same disease and died even younger, and one night her ghost came to him in a dream, and she was looking for her dolls, and he'd locked them all away in a chest in the attic, and the very next morning, he sat them in the windows so she'd see them right away if she ever came back. One day last spring, Pauline told me she was moving to Florida, that she'd been taking classes in Spiritualism at the place on the coast and had heard about a whole community of Spiritualists who live together in a town in Florida. "So you won't see me here much longer," she said. "After my daughter finishes the school year, we're moving there. I wouldn't want you to think I'd been fired or anything. I'm going there to study. Try and become a medium myself. So I can help other people talk to their loved ones like I've been able to talk to my mom and dad." Then she leaned over the counter, closer to me, even though no one else was around. "I hear you lost your husband," she said. "If you ever want to talk to him, let me know. I'm here to the end of June. I can try to contact him." I gave her my little bow. After that I sent Genko to the post office. Until the end of June.

Anyway, it shows I'm not the only one who talks to ghosts.

And there's our neighbor, Lucy. I've told you about her before. So beautiful, in her strangeness. One night last summer she told me that sometimes, when she thinks about her late mother, something comes over her and things get shiny and the air starts to hum like bees. That's how she put it. And then the things she usually thinks are real—she sees that they're not real at all. That the whole world is pretending.

I wish I could have told her I understand. Not because you make the world shiny. Or that I hear bees. But because of how it happens. How I never go looking for it, either. Even the very first time, the day we got here, when Genko was fixing up his room and I came out to the back

52

yard. Sure I was thinking about you. When am I not? But I wasn't conjuring you, any more than Lucy tries to conjure her mother. All the same, there you were, walking right up out of the pond and smiling.

Like you're smiling now. Which makes me think you haven't become a wanderer. Or a hungry ghost. But why haven't you moved on?

Are you waiting for me to remarry, have another child? Then you could come back as Genko's half-brother. Or sister. Maybe you made your parents send me that letter. The one I got yesterday. They said I should find happiness with someone new. "We hope you are getting out and meeting others in your village. Genko needs a father. Ren would want him to have a father." But think about it, Ren. What kind of man would want a burned, mute wife?

A burned, mute wife who's not a widow.

They also said—again—that they can't understand why I left California. They say that every letter. Last year I sent them photos of Genko buying apples, Genko in the pumpkin patch, Genko making a snowman and skating on the pond. But they still don't seem to understand. "We'd like to visit," they say, "but you're so far away." What's another few hours, though, when you're flying from Japan?

I suspect they blame me. They're too polite ever to say so. But they blame me. To hell with the settlement. To hell with my burns. I rescued Genko and myself. That's how they see it. Understandably. It gives them something to hold onto.

Still, I wish they were more a part of Genko's life. Of course my parents adore him, but it's not the same. He needs his Japanese family, his Japanese heritage.

I know. We could as well go to Japan. And we will.

When I'm ready.

Have I ever told you about the time—it was last fall—I went online and did a search on "Japanese in Maine"? The first hit I got was a list of Japanese restaurants. Then I got a listing of towns with the largest percentage of Japanese residents. Number one was a place on the Blue Hill Peninsula. I forget the name. The percentage of Japanese was 1.25.

Okay, I thought, it's not much. But if this town has, say, 3,000 residents, then that means there's maybe 36 or 37 Japanese people there. Might be worth a visit. Then I had the brilliant idea to look up the population of the place. You know what it was? Eighty. Eighty people. Meaning one Japanese person lives there. That weekend I took Genko to a Japanese restaurant in Brunswick. It was good. You'd have liked it. One of the waiters reminded me of you.

Sort of.

Not really.

Anyway, the point is, I'm not interested.

I'm not free.

Because of you.

And even if I were, how would I go about finding this father for Genko? Just for a start, how many eligible bachelors know sign language?

Doctor Viv wants me to see a speech pathologist. She thinks maybe I could talk again. She doesn't understand how hard it is to make any sound at all. And when I do, like this morning, it's so ugly. Like a pig grunting.

Sometimes before I go to sleep, I put on my headphones and listen to music. Eva Cassidy, for instance. "Autumn Leaves" or "Ain't No Sunshine." I mouth the words and pretend it's me. Singing to you.

Last night, though, I listened to Adele. "Set Fire to the Rain." Probably not the smartest choice. I had the nightmare again. Running down the stairs, holding Genko, screaming at you to wake up.

I swear I screamed, Ren.

I screamed and screamed.

The coroner said you were probably already overcome with smoke. That you probably never woke up at all. I didn't tell him—I never told anyone—about the Ambien. Or that we'd been arguing. Or that sleep was always your way of tuning me out.

You must remember what the argument was about. Aren't ghosts supposed to know such things? Was it something about Genko? Or money?

Was it my fault?

Do you remember?

If you do, why won't you tell me?

Of course it still matters.

It just does. To me. I think about it all the time. That and the endless chain of all those seemingly trivial antecedents. Whatever one or the other of us said or did that started the argument. A couple of pills. Genko begging for one more chapter of *Harry Potter*. Frayed wires. Sparks. Cheap insulation.

All of it essential. Not a single piece expendable.

If we hadn't argued, the smoke alarm would have woken you up, like it did me, and we'd have days now when maybe we wouldn't remember the fire even once. Or maybe we'd remember it every time we wanted to speak to each other and couldn't, but at least we'd be burned and mute together.

And when we got angry, we'd argue in signs. Or throw vegetables at each other. And when we were sorry and wanted to make up, we'd ring the bell.

Instead of which, I argue with you and you just sit there. A smile. That's all I get. You might as well have stayed away permanently.

I mean it, Ren. I don't want to live this way.

Everyone keeps telling me I have to forgive myself. Doctor Viv, for instance. *Jenny, you mustn't blame yourself!*

Why mustn't I? You do.

I'm like a maiden in a fairy tale locked in a fortress room waiting for you to say the magic words that will break the spell.

But you never say them. Every day, just when I think we're getting somewhere, up you get, turn your back, and walk away again, down the path to the pond. And you swim out, all the way out to the horizon, and disappear again. In silence.

Yours, I mean. Not just mine.

It's torture, isn't it?

You're torturing me. Punishing me.

Why don't you send another fire?

You can send a fish, for sure you can send a few sparks.

Or maybe I go for a swim and get some sort of cramp and drown. You could manage a little thing like that, couldn't you? Or what about poisonous mushrooms? A rusty nail? Black ice on the road?

Or maybe you just want to haunt me till everyone thinks I've lost my mind and they put me away?

Okay, forget it. Anyway, it's nearly time for the school bus.

Aren't you leaving?

Leave, Ren. Just leave.

I'll walk you down to the water. Past your gruesome little fish.

Hah. Too late. That osprey's about to make your fish his meal . . . or his wife's meal. She's been brooding for weeks.

There he goes. See? He's given it to her. Even though he's smaller than she is. And so active. He's got to be hungry.

You remember that hike we took at Wolfe's Neck? We were visiting my parents. Genko was just a baby—I remember I was carrying him in his sling. And we saw an osprey flying to his nest with a big fish in his claws, and that ranger said male mortality is high because he defends the nest and brings the mother food long after the chicks have hatched.

And you reached down and held me, Ren.

You held us both. Circled us with your arms.

I could feel your warmth like a little cocoon all around us, and I rested my cheek against your chest.

And you told me . . .

You told me . . .

What did you tell me? I've forgotten, Ren. What did you tell me? What did you say?

We stood there a long time, didn't we? Maybe we were thinking about the ospreys, or our marriage, or our son. Or maybe we were thinking about having dinner that night with my parents, or getting on the plane back to California the next day, or your job or mine.

But we couldn't have been thinking—because we didn't know—that somewhere, far away, was an old house we'd never seen, a house with old wires, where someday an old woman would fall, and her children would move her to a nursing home, and they'd rent the house out, and we'd happen to see the advertisement tacked up to the board at our favorite coffee shop, and we'd move there, and we'd sleep there, and someday—no, some cold night—I'd burn and you'd die there.

If we had known that, Ren. If only we could have known.

What? Would we have loved each other more?

How much more love is there than a shared bed, for instance? A son, for instance? Thousands of meals, books, letters, emails, photographs, sinks scrubbed, leaves raked, good mornings, good nights, arguments, sleeping pills, loss, grief, regret?

Remember I asked that ranger, *What if the osprey's mate dies?*

And the answer? "Oh, she'll find someone new. Probably the following spring. When it's time to breed again."

But you and I aren't birds, Ren. Maybe I should write and point that out to your parents. That you're . . . a memory. And I'm . . . What am I, Ren?

One who remembers.

And I do remember.

I remember you told me that you loved us. That you would love us forever. Not "until death do us part," but forever. That's what you said.

And I'd forgotten it.

And you sent me the fish to remind me. The fish that dropped from the sky and died in my hands and was taken by an osprey to his nest and reminded me of a day so infinitely long ago when you told me you'd love us forever.

I'm sorry I'd forgotten it, Ren. I'd ask you to forgive me, but . . . whatever once wanted forgiveness is gone. So I'll just thank you.

For this moment. The ospreys. The sunlight. Your smile. Dazzling as ever.

And see? I'm smiling, too.

Go. It's all right. We'll be all right.
We love each other now.
We love each other forever.
We let each other go.

Without Apology
Becca Shaw Glaser

I'm going to write a sweet poem.
I don't care if they're not in fashion.

I won't be ashamed to love the world, to like lady's mantle
or usnea moss stuck to a stick.

I want to remember in kindergarten how we learned to pour
blue and red water together to make purple, or counted with beans,
beat butter from cream.

I licked pesto off plates, ate strawberry shortcake
handmade by my mama. She read us kid's books, changing
them so the passive girl characters got to do cool stuff.
Nightly she sang us lullabies,
rubbing our small, anxious backs.

I love the usual things—
the fat moon pinned to the sky, my imperfect family—
my beautiful brothers with their
shaved cheeks, bald heads, curled toes.

When I tell my brother I had to drag
myself out of bed he suggests an aquarium:
If you find any animals, put them in there. You need creatures to tend.

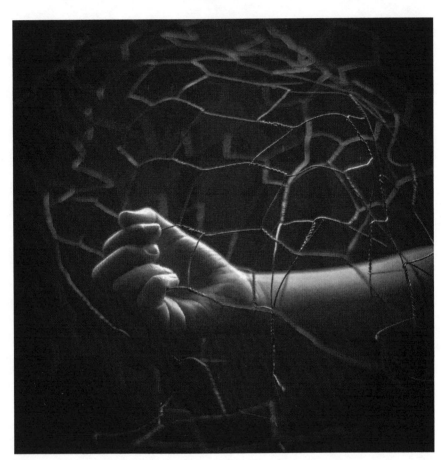

Magnolia at the Farm, 2022, by Amy Wilton

Tidying Up
Ellen Baker

"'The way life should be,' hmm?" she said. The billboard had promised it on their arrival three days ago—but now, trying to leave, they were stuck in traffic. Who could imagine—a traffic jam in Maine? A single line of cars, crawling for an hour, each just waiting to cross this narrow bridge over this sprawling tidal river. The only way out, Siri had claimed. And why wouldn't he put up the top, turn on the A/C, keep his foot on the brake like a normal person? No. He was using the clutch and gas to rock the Miata back and forth—each time nearly kissing the *HELL NO GMO* bumper sticker on the rusty Outback they were stuck behind. Trying to read was hopeless. She stuffed her copy of *The Life-Changing Magic of Tidying Up* into her overflowing beach bag, yanked out her pink sunhat and put it on. People who envied people in convertibles had never ridden in one.

"I was told traffic lets up across the bridge," he said. "Just after Red's Eats. Seems the whole world lines up there for the lobster rolls. Wreaks havoc."

"You optimist, you."

It was supposed to have been a romantic weekend, accommodations and plans presented as a surprise for her birthday six weeks ago. Anticipation and bawdy promises about nude swimming had turned to fog and Scrabble and a lighthouse jigsaw puzzle. The ocean, twelve feet from their door, was for forty-eight hours invisible through the blear. "It's actually *nice*, the sound of the waves and the birds and the rain," she'd said sunnily, wounding him enough that he—a reader of Homer and Chekov and Dostoyevsky who believed nothing good had been written since 1934—went to the living room, snatched a dog-eared copy of *A*

Game of Thrones off the crooked shelf and didn't come to bed till past two. This morning, when they'd had to pack up to join the hordes heading back south, the sun had broken through like a demented joke.

"You could hop out," he said, "run up there to Red's, stand in line for a couple lobster rolls. You'd probably have them in hand by the time I got there with the car."

She pictured it: Everyone in every car in this single-file line, scrutinizing her rear end—four sizes too big this summer. Even her flowing skirt couldn't camouflage it. "I ate so much lobster already, I belong in a trap," she said. The one dream of the weekend that had come true: lobster at every meal. In retrospect, not a great idea.

They were halfway across. The water glimmered below. She saw she'd gotten chocolate on her shirt, a remnant of the roadside ice cream stand they'd stopped at in a last stab at salvaging "summer fun." Was this what middle age was? Spilling things without noticing?

He flipped on the radio and started scanning. Past the classical and talk. Past Led Zeppelin, some cowboy with a broken heart. When the first strains of "Harder to Breathe" came through, she started semi-dancing in her seat, shoulders shimmying, hands pumping to the beat.

He shut off the radio. Gave a tiny NPR-listener sniff.

He had that way of acting like he was the whole world.

Sometimes she rewound her life and played it fast-forward again, tallying evidence. Six months after her divorce, she'd congratulated herself on meeting someone she thought she could talk to. A year in, he'd adopted a churlish cat who wouldn't let her into the bedroom. Quarrels ensued. Sides were taken. Resentments brewed and lingered. Seven pet-psychic sessions later, all cat demands met, she moved in. His townhouse was twenty years old, in a cul-de-sac of a dozen others all alike. ("I guess you like beige," she'd said, the first time she'd visited. "Taupe," he corrected her.) Then, one day, he arrived home in the Miata. "Surprise!" he said. He'd traded in his Volvo wagon. She accused him of a mid-life crisis. "Have some imagination," he said.

His daughter had never liked her. Her son called him "Dweebman." Holidays were a chore. Three Christmases and she hadn't once gotten her way, not even about the tinsel. (Again, the cat could be blamed.)

She perched her bare feet on the dash, arranging her skirt to spare herself the sight of the tiny varicose vein that had popped up—as if by clockwork—the week after her birthday. Her calculations on whether to have the hideous thing fixed involved complicated ratios of vanity, her bank account, her position on actuarial tables. She was fifty-three now. Things required more thought.

The Outback loomed—

"Brake!" she yelled. He stomped. A small whiplash.

He laughed. "Good thing *one* of us is paying attention!"

She let out her breath. Smiled. She liked that he didn't get mad about silly things the way her ex-husband would have, or blame her for his mistakes. Anyway, it wasn't the end of the world, this business with the clutch and the gas. Even the Miata in general was really fine. Even the *cat.* Here was a man who liked the ballet! Who quoted works of literature like other people quoted their fathers. He might be three inches too short, but he did have the shiny black hair and thick beard of a much younger man. Anyway, at her age—her mother often reminded her— she'd been lucky to find someone.

"You sweet man." She put her hand on his thigh. "Thank you for my birthday weekend, complete with fog."

Silence. The car, rocking up and back, up and back. She'd be seasick soon, she thought.

"Hello?" A light squeeze.

"I just. . . " Behind his sunglasses, his face squinched up.

Suspicion made her reel in her hand. They were almost to the end of the bridge. The crowd at Red's. She could feel the heat of sunburn beginning on her arms. She'd been too late putting on her hat. Her nose would look like one of those lobsters. Boiled. "You what?"

He sighed, a sudden victim. "I have to *try* so hard. With you."

She glanced away. She could make out the placid faces in the long line at Red's, suppliants waiting for redemption. Others—emanating the relief of the already-forgiven—gathered around picnic tables, eating and laughing in the sun.

She thought she could get past this. This *moment*—with him. She forced a laugh. "Well! A thousand pardons. I'll try to make your life easy-peasy from now on."

"Like that! I'm trying to be serious, here." He turned toward her, sunglasses glinting, then looked straight ahead at the Outback. "This probably seems to come out of nowhere."

"Darling. Why don't you be specific? I can't read your mind," she said, then was proud to have masked her revving panic. Though there seemed to be a current now, pulling them toward a falls.

"Look, I guess I've just been forcing it," he said. "These last weeks. The deposit on that place was non-refundable." Another sniff. "Anyway, it was for your birthday."

A sudden gust of wind blew her pink hat off. She swiveled to watch it fly over the rail. A tall boy—one of the Red's picnickers—gave chase as it cruised over the mud flats. When it settled on the water, he stopped, shrugged up at her in an outsized way. A distant figure with good intentions. She waved her thanks and stayed with her feet on the dash, watching the pink shape bobbing. Floating out to sea.

Convertibles were mistakes on wheels. She supposed that boy, though, wished *he* might be going somewhere in a sporty car—somewhere he'd dream up as better than any place his own life promised. But she imagined being him. Everything out ahead. Never having to compromise.

Octobers
Alexandra S.D. Hindrichs

There are apples
   and cinnamon
      and wars.
Stir as I might
   they settle into separate
heaps of bitter
    sweet
  spice
startling red leaves
whole trees
bursting into flame
   matchsticks
and the salt laden tears of a girl
   I don't know
(but do)
for the fire's in her, too.
So much has burned
while I
   an ocean of weeping away
flip pages
   frustrate over the timing of
a door shut,
a text sent
muddy
   soccer fields
when sky promised sun
   even my annoyances
are but sticky honey jar lids
extravagant.

I think of her, though,
    I do.
Of her fears firing like gunshot
    opening like wounds
        blooming like blood
of the bravery she's forced into
stiff, tight, ill-fitting and exquisite
    as it becomes mundane
        like oats
in this season of apples.
    I want to send her the crisp
tangy taste
    in baskets:
here is nothing
    helpful
    but maybe
maybe
    you could hurl them
smash
then bite.
Here is patient
    dooming
        hope.
I have nutmeg, too.

Ferry Terminal, Lincolnville, by Jim Nickelson

More than I Could Know
Jeffrey C. Lewis

The Graves is a jagged rock ledge off the coast of Maine that is barely visible when the tide is high. A Coast Guard bell buoy warns of its location, tolling with the swells. The ring is more clunky than clear, and with the gurgling of waves surging over kelp and rocks, the sound is lonely and cold even on a warm, calm day. Some say that a hundred ships have wrecked there, but I've never seen evidence for any of them and I'm not sure I believe what people say.

I'm thinking about the Graves because I'm thinking about Easter. I have a sermon to write and I'm not sure how to approach that same old story about an empty grave. Easter is coming late this year, as is spring itself. I shouldn't be surprised. That's the way spring always comes to Maine, reluctantly and late, after several false starts. As I work in a boatyard and pastor a small island church, the relationship of Easter to springtime can be confusing. I heard a lobsterman contemptuously call a mild day in late March "fake spring." The apparent benevolence of clement weather cannot be trusted too soon.

Easter is a moveable feast, meaning it has no fixed date from year to year. By convention, it begins at sundown on the evening of the first Sunday, after the first full moon, after the vernal equinox. The astronomical movements behind the date are as predictable as the tides. But in Maine, the promise of spring takes its time. On any given year the calendar may say that spring has arrived weeks before the weather consents to it. The lingering cold makes it hard to believe in the season.

Easter sermons have been hard for me in the past. One reason is the temptation of trying to say too much, or trying to explain an event that is beyond belief for many who come to church only once or twice a year. Over the years I've to settled into an approach for the high holy days when the church is extra full: Stay out of the way of the stories. Let them speak for themselves. Whatever anyone believes about Easter, or doesn't, or can't, I believe that some stories work on us, even change us, just by encountering them.

Easter is a season, not just a day; it's a full seven weeks long. Perhaps the strands of the story need time to sink in, like oil brushed into wooden oars. Miracle stories are hard to absorb, even for the people who were in them. On that first Easter morning when the women went to the grave to anoint the scourged, battered, pierced body of Jesus, they found the tomb was empty. Their response was not to claim victory and sing, "Alleluia!" No! Far from it. Confused and scared, they went away without telling anyone. No one called the empty grave a miracle.

What is a miracle? It seems like a simple enough question. Miracles are always good. There are no bad or depressing miracles. Miracles are joyful even if they bring tears. Miracles are surprising and unexpected. They always produce gratitude that can't be explained. And they are always hard to believe. They are, by definition, incredible—that is, not credible, not believable. Just as trials need credible witnesses to make the exercise of discerning justice legitimate, stories need believability for us to find them acceptable or useful for our lives. If we cannot accept them, they are merely preposterous. A preposterous event will never make us grateful.

I know from putting God on trial in the courts of my skeptical mind that miracle stories can be troubling. They ask too much of us. Did Jesus really make a blind man see by rubbing spit-soaked dirt on his eyes? Did a dead little girl really come back to life after Jesus told her parents she was just sleeping? Such stories rasped at my sense of reason and my experience of life. But even worse, they offended my yearning for the goodness of God. If I could believe in a god was who is all good and all powerful, then God had a lot to answer for in abiding the unspeakable atrocities of history. I became aware of this problem when I was ten and one of my best friends died tragically. The look of grief on his mother's face scared me, and I realized that I had a serious issue with God. I could not express it rationally, but I knew in my young bones that there was a problem. I didn't know this had a name until decades later and I was studying theology two days a week while working in a boatyard for three. Theologians, I learned, had a name for this problem—how believers could reconcile a good and all-powerful God with the presence of so much evil and suffering in the world. In the dictionary of theological terms it was called *theodicy*. In the boatyard, I silently referred to it with my secret acronym: *WTFG?*

Theodicy remained one of the perennial challenges in the work list of my life. Like old wooden boats that leak, always, it was a problem I had to learn to live with. I've been wrestling with it since I was ten, the age many kids start to give up their belief in Santa Claus and the Easter Bunny. I thought I solved it by giving up on God and even the idea of "God." But that didn't work either. Life had its problems that the forsaking of God did not solve. But I did not have the right tools or the right stories to resolve all the tensions of doubt and faith once and for all. They go together. Like a floating boat that leaks, I can live with it, especially when the boat makes my life so much better than my life would be without it.

In the boatyard I heard a saying about the difference between fairy tales and sea stories. Fairy tales always begin with "Once upon a time." But sea stories start with, "No shit, this really happened." Like any honest skeptic I both suffered the temptation to see some Bible stories as something akin to fairy tales. The culture I grew up in, immersed in like water, made this virtually impossible not to do. But when I dared to stand in the pulpit and gazed into the sea of eyes waiting to hear good news, the tension of honesty and doubt could be agonizing when I struggled to believe the story. This is every preacher's moment of truth. Stay out of the way and tell the story true. What I am about to tell you really happened.

On a Saturday in the season of Easter my middle son decided to go sailing, alone. He was eighteen years old at the time, a kind of Melvillian "Billy Budd" character who reminds me of the salty swagger I still cherish from when I was a lad. An accomplished sailor, he had already completed two trans-Atlantic sailing voyages, one of them with me. He was just returning to Maine after wandering around Europe alone.

A gusty north wind raced down over the coastal mountains and out over the cold water and the rocky islands and ledges in the bay. That he decided to go sailing was not surprising. He sailed alone often throughout his youth, just as his older brother had done, and just as I had done, more times than it's possible to remember.

One of my friends told me once that my wife and I raised our boys as if they were growing up in the 1970s, that is, without much supervision. That is not totally true, but I accept it as a fair assessment in comparison to the safety culture that emerged when our boys came into the world. We had a symbiotic tension in our parenting, pulling in different directions as mother and father. Her "Be careful" tightened my "See if you can climb higher." This tension attested to the truth that we both loved them. We tended to have a light hand on the tiller of their lives, encouraging them into experiences where consequences for mistakes could be real. This was not because we did not love them and did not care if they got hurt. The truth is more like the opposite. We loved them so much that we yearned for them to live fully with abundant lives, not paralyzed with an over-abundance of our control over them. We had our eyes on them when they climbed trees or leaped off ledges into cold water. But we gave them space to be boys with as much adventure as they could take in. We trusted that their little adventures would provide them judgement and courage for the days to come when we would not be there.

The days came when we would not be there arrived, and on one of those days the boy went sailing, alone, on a brisk spring day. No one else was out. Though the offshore wind had a tease of spring in it, the ocean was still very cold. The boat had been in my family since I was young. We all know that a sailboat is a thing, an inanimate object. And yet, with vessels like the *Scaffie*, there is more to it. Somehow it feels not untrue to say that this boat is an old friend- and a member of the family.

She has nice lines, as boat people say. Her form and function join in

71

a graceful harmony that is just lovely, whether tied to the dock or underway with three boys and the family dog. Even lubbers who don't know boats see that she is beautiful with her sinuous shape and traditional rig. She wears the compliment "big little boat" well, meaning that she is uncommonly seaworthy and stout, even though she is just shy of fifteen feet long. There are much larger boats I trust much less.

She can be rowed or sailed, and with her open hull design (meaning she has no deck) she is roomy, like a big cradle. Her single sail is tanbark red—warm and salty, the color of the blood-stained canvass on fishing schooners from another age.

The *Scaffie* and her single crew raced by the empty moorings, then jibed to head south on a starboard tack after passing the lighthouse at the seaward end of the harbor. Everything was great. Then, strangely, the breeze just died. A sudden lull can bring an ominous pause, as the boat slows and stands upright, as if snapping to attention. This got Tristan's attention and he eased the sail and took a step toward the mast, to be more ready for whatever change was coming—or not.

Then the whole world changed. The wind came back from a different direction, over forty knots of it. The cold sudden blast swatted the rig from the other side of the sail, immediately capsizing the *Scaffie* and casting Tristan into the frigid sea. She completely "turned turtle," her mast pointing straight into the deep, her keel exposed to the wind, awash on the surface, barely. The water was turgid and biting. Tristan was not wearing his life jacket.

I did not know any of this. For I was on the other side of the continent, in California, with my wife and youngest son, Alden. Ironically, we were at a swim meet. Alden was competing with his high school team. The day was calm and bright on the central coast, but you could not call it warm. The Pacific is cold there and the damp chill reached up into the hills. Everyone wore sweaters or jackets. Even the swimmers wore their long team coats, bouncing on the deck to stay warm until it was their turn to climb onto the starting blocks to take their mark .

Alden held onto the edge of the pool, panting with the other swimmers, after finishing the 100-meter breaststroke. He was shivering and his lips were blue.

That's when my phone buzzed in my pocket. I would not have taken the call from the unknown number had it not been for the 207 area-code on the screen. Maine.

"Hello?"

"Hello, this is Lt. Richard DerBoghosian from the Maine Marine Patrol. Is this Mr. Lewis? I'm calling about the marine incident today."

I said nothing. Time was needed for what I'd just heard to sink in.

"Marine incident? What?"

"Do you have a boat in Camden Harbor?" the stranger asked.

"Yeah, well, sort of . . . I mean, I'm in California, but we have a little boat we keep at the town dock in Camden."

"Do you know about the incident today?"

With this question, a wave of dread swamped me, and I was scared. Words came out like a squall, and they blew out in the form of an order: "You need to tell me what is going on."

"I'm sorry," said the voice, recalibrating. "It seems that your son was involved in a marine incident this morning. Apparently, he was taken to Penobscot Bay Medical Center. Do you know anything about this?"

I did not.

The pool deck was bright—and loud—with hundreds of chattering voices, making it difficult to hear. I pressed the phone hard to my head, bewildered. Water was everywhere. A cold weight squeezed my chest and my vision got blurry with a new flood of water in my eyes. Alden sprang from the pool as limber as a seal lion, wrapped himself in a warm towel and joined his teammates on the deck.

It's hard to swim with all your clothes on. When the boat went over, Tristan was wearing jeans, a hooded sweatshirt, and a heavy work jacket. Also, of course, his worn Vans skateboarding shoes. Shoes make it even harder to swim.

It hurts to think about the cold heaviness of his clothes. I see him scrambling onto the overturned hull. Somehow, he wrestles the *Scaffie* back to upright and pulls himself into the swamped cradle full of cold water, as wind-whipped waves wash over the rails. The wind howls. The sail smacks and whips as he un-cleats the halyard with his shaking hands to drop the rig before the wind capsizes the boat again.

He needs get to the urgent work of bailing out the water. The world is suddenly primal, essential, serious, and cold. The only reason the boat did not sink was the hidden foam infused inside interior pockets of the hull. When the boat flipped, one of the oars floated out and blew away downwind, as did the bailing bucket. He'd have to retrieve the bucket to have any chance at bailing out the water. And so he does this, swimming with all his clothes on in the cold wind and spray.

The truth of the story took a long time to come to my wife and me, and it came to us in waves.

Having retrieved the bucket, but unable to get the lost oar, he got back to relative safety of the boat to set about re-floating her. He bailed and bailed and bailed, shivering. But the *Scaffie* had settled so low in the sea that the waves kept washing over the gunwales. Each bucketful of seawater Tristan sent back into the ocean with his cold hands was immediately replaced as the incessant whitecaps breached the sides of the boat.

The situation revealed itself to be futile. And scary, and cold, and getting worse. He could not sail the swamped boat back to the harbor. He could not row it against the wind with only one oar. His inability to bail out the water became dire. Being alone made it worse. He had no radio. His phone, soaked in his jacket pocket and didn't work. He could not have pushed the buttons to call for help even if it did.

The shivering of his body was fierce. His clothes were heavy, cold, and wet. His hands were numb and clumsy. With each passing second, the north wind stripped his body of its precious little heat, as it whipped up the waves that thwarted his efforts to bail. The direction of the wind was an extra menace, relentlessly blowing him and the *Scaffie* further offshore. The further out they drifted the larger the waves grew.

No one saw any of this. No one else was out sailing that day. Add that to the list of considerations that might have guided his decision to sail in the first place, but that's not even close to the main point of the story.

"Never leave the boat" is closer. The ocean is merciless if you don't have something to float in or on. Even a swamped boat is floating some —and floating some is a whole universe away from not floating at all. I cannot possibly convey the seriousness of the fundamental adage about never leaving the boat until you have another one to get into. And even then, as another saying goes, "You step *up*(not down) into a life raft." Never leave the boat before you have to.

There are stories about the judgment of God. But I don't think that God, however "God" is conceived, could be as ruthless as the dispassionate indifference of nature. Nature does not care about little boats upon the ocean or the souls alive in them. The laws that describe thermodynamics, convection, biochemistry, metabolism, respiration, or fluid dynamics can make the consequences for decisions and mistakes harder and colder than any parent's willingness to describe.

Of course my son could have avoided the whole disaster by doing anything else that day. He could have gone skateboarding. He could have watched YouTube videos in the warm house. He could have gone for a hike up the mountain with his guitar. His guitar, by the way, as I found out over a year later, was on the boat with him. It scudded off in the wind, along with the oar, when the boat capsized.

While one son shivered with friends at the pool, the other son, lashed by the ruthless judgment of nature, faced a terrible decision.

Blowing offshore fast, he had made no progress in his fight to bail out the *Scaffie*. Terribly cold and getting colder, his body started to shut down. He knew that no help was coming. He knew he was going to die.

If he stayed with the boat, his body might be found in the wreckage, washed up on one of the offshore islands or ledges. *If.* At the direction he was drifting, *if* he did not wash up on an island or ledge, the next hard stop was Africa. Knowing the truth of his inevitable death if he stayed with the boat, he made the final decision to leave the *Scaffie*, to take the chance of swimming for his life. If his life was to end that day, he would at least die trying to get closer to home, not drifting away, not waiting.

He put on the lifejacket that miraculously had not blown away. Then he lowered himself into the frigid waves and let go of the rail. The *Scaffie* would blow out to sea, and he would swim away from her, against the same wind that knocked her down and changed everything about the day. He told himself that once he left the boat, he would not turn back, not matter how scared or cold he got. This was his decision.

Of all the "wrong" decisions he made, the hardest of them was the one that allows me to tell this story at all. His decision forced me to be careful with my judgments. I am not free of them, but I have become more sober and more careful with their application.

The Gulf of Maine oceanographic data for that day is stark. The water in Penobscot Bay was in the low forties Fahrenheit. The wind was out of the northwest fifteen to twenty-five, with higher gusts, some above forty miles per hour. I've also studied the hypothermia charts that describe in dispassionate detail what happens when a person is suddenly cast into water of that temperature. Urgent and involuntary gasps for air ensue instantly. In five minutes or fewer, dexterity of the body wanes, first with numbness and then followed with complete loss of control—of fingers, hands, limbs, and speech. In thirty to sixty minutes, exhaustion gives way to unconsciousness. In less than an hour, but in no case longer than three, death is inevitable.

Some ocean swimmers achieve daunting feats of endurance in cold water. But these athletes are marvels of adaptation and practice. They train themselves to stretch beyond normal bounds of human performance. These exceptions reveal the general rules of human biology. Other people swallow swords and breath fire. Some ride six-foot unicycles and juggle chainsaws. All of these are emblematic of the wondrous achievements of the human mind, body, and spirit. These are marvelous, impressive, amazing, even incredible. But no one would call them miracles.

Tristan made the decision he knew that he was never supposed to make. He left the boat to try to swim for shore. Years later, this memory remains tender for him and for my wife and me. The longest part of the story cannot be told, not by me anyway. But I'll say it again: He swam away from the boat. He swam, against the wind, into the incessant onslaught of waves, heavy in his frigid clothes, toward land.

He swam and swam and swam. The waves in his face were cruel with their sting until his skin went numb. But then a new pain was even worse, deep, and dull and heavy. But nothing lasts forever. The dull pain faded, and shivers eventually ceased. A calming lull of profound and comforting peace surrounded him, and he began to forgive himself for the series of decisions that led him to that moment. He had tried his best and felt a warm affirmation—or was it a welcome?—that, somehow, that truth was known.

But like the lull before the capsize, this one was ended when a blunt terror seized him with the worst thought he'd ever had. A phone call to his parents... Someone had found a body.... "We think it might be your son. We are sorry." The cold and pain were back, and worse than before.

The terror of the thought ended the peace. That was when he took off his shoes and resolved to kick harder than he thought was possible. He turned onto his back, his head immersed in the icy water, looking only at the sky as he kicked his way, fiercely, slowly, into the wind, toward the shore he could not see.

The story took weeks to emerge in a shape that my wife and I could believe. Brothers talked to each other with details not shared with parents. Strands of what happened floated back to us like flotsam washing ashore after a storm. Some pieces came directly from Tristan, some from his brothers, some from friends who reported details of what they'd heard about what happened on that day. Not everything we heard was true and not everything true needs to be said.

But I'm happy to tell you: he reached the shore.

The rocks were cold and jagged, and he could not feel his feet as he crawled over them. That part of the coast is steep and bold. His legs did not work anymore. He could not stand. And yet, somehow, he crawled up the rocks and into the woods. He must have. Because eventually he arrived at a house—a huge summer house. But it was still far from summer. No one would be there for many weeks.

And yet, there was a carpenter there that day. On a Saturday. I don't I know why he was working at the house on that Saturday that spring. But it was a very good thing he came to work. The goodness in his going to work that day was more than he could know. He was inside when a thump landed on the door.

When the carpenter opened it, a young man lay there, wet, and barefoot and unable to speak. When my son tried to ask for help, there were no words, just slurred sounds of air escaping through failing muscles. The carpenter got the wet clothes off the lad and put his own coat on him. He had a wool blanket in his truck. He got Tristan to the truck and wrapped him in his blanket. Leaving his work and tools, he raced down the coast highway to get the boy to the hospital.

Later my phone buzzed with 207 as I stood on a pool deck in California cheering my son Alden in a swimming race.

We did not hear Tristan's voice until darkness had fallen from Maine to California, after he'd been released from the hospital. He called us from a land line. From the other side of the continent, we huddled around his voice coming out of the little speaker in the bottom of my phone, holding it like treasure.

Unfortunately, because we are parents, our gratitude was contaminated with a flurry of incredulous questions. Questions, like: "Did you have a reef in?" "Did you tell anyone you were going out?" "How much was it blowing when you left the dock?" I'll never forget the still firmness of his response to the last one, answering to his parents respectfully, humbly, but centered on an even keel: "Dad, when you wind up in the hospital near death with hypothermia, you pretty much know you fucked up."

After those words, I ceased with the inquisition. Almost. There was just one detail I was dying to know. I needed—I just needed to know—one thing: Where, exactly, was he?

"When you capsized, were you outside the island or in the gut between the lighthouse and the mainland?"

"Outside."

Then: "When you made the decision to leave the boat, how far out were you?"

"Dad, I don't want to tell you that."

I could only respond with silence and tears he could not see from the coast of another ocean.

It is a blessing when brothers talk with each other. And it is a blessing that they don't share everything with their old man. I had my private estimates about where Tristan must have been, and how long he must have been in the water, because I needed to make sense of what happened. I needed to be able to believe it. In one conversation with our oldest son I told him that Tristan was lucky to be alive, for I figured he was swimming for over half an hour before he reached the shore. This was an astounding and terrifying fact for a dad to consider. Upon hearing my incredulous estimate, the older brother took a breath—and after a pause sighed, "Oh, Dad, he was in the water for a lot longer than that."

Some events reveal a well of gratitude that is so deep it's beyond belief. This story really happened, and it had a happy ending. And yet, my incredulous skepticism cannot fully absorb that it was real.

One of the men in my life who floats in that precious place as my friend as well as a friend to my sons, told me a piece of the story a year later. He had his own questions, born not of a father's need for cross-examination, but as a fellow sailor who wanted to learn from an experience he hopes never to have. He shared a response to one of his questions because he loved Tristan's answer, and he wanted our family to hear it. "What were you thinking about when you swam toward shore?"

"I just thought how I wanted to see my mom and dad and my brothers again."

The Coast Guard found the boat, drifting upright but swamped several miles out to sea. Her registration sticker on the bow revealed the home harbor. The crew pumped her out and towed her back, and secured her to the town dock, where Tristan had untied her to go for a sail. The harbormaster called me to share news that the *Scaffie* was back. I asked him some details that he confirmed. The oars were gone. The thwarts (benches) were gone. The anchor was gone. "No, I didn't see any bag of life jackets," he said. But the red sail was there, collapsed and lying unfurled in the bottom of the boat, like an unmade bed in a boy's room.

The marine incident report came to me months later where it came to rest in a folder on my desk. It was written by Lt. DerBoghosian, the man who called me in California, when he knew very little, and I knew nothing. He got the details straight from my son after he was released from the hospital. The report is clear, professional, appropriate, true—and cold. It cannot convey the depth of what mattered most in what did and did not happen that day. If you can say that anything about the bureaucratic report was warm, that warmth was in the names.

The hospital told the Maine Marine Patrol and the US Coast Guard the name of the carpenter who went to work that day—the man who answered the door in the empty summer house. The boat and my son are still in my life for a stranger helped save him. I tried for months to find Shawn. My wife and I wanted to share with him our immense gratitude. We thanked God he came to work that day and answered the door.

After many on-line searches and dead-end phone calls, my search to find and thank the carpenter ended suddenly. His name was Shawn. A story in the local paper told of a single car accident with a tree and a sharp turn on a windy country road. There was a name and a photograph along with the short story in the paper. When I showed Tristan the picture, he said, "Yeah, that's him." When I told him what happened his face dropped. I could see the ocean in his eyes when he hugged me and said he had to take a walk. I sat in the chair and cried.

Someday, Tristan may share the fullness of the words that Shawn told him on the cold drive to the hospital. He shared something of the essence of them with me, but I know I won't get them right. I'll just hold to the spirit of what I heard. Shawn survived a hard and abusive childhood. As an adult he had been in trouble with the law, with many years in prison. But he'd found faith—or faith found him—and he was not afraid to tell Tristan on the way to the hospital that he gave thanks to God for saving him. "Just so you know, Tristan, that is the Bible," pointing the book on dashboard. There is goodness more than you can know.

I have nowhere to put this story except in a holy place in heaven where profound sadness and endless gratitude are held together.

With the first day of spring came a lovely morning with light south wind and air temperature in the low sixties. Tristan and I sailed out to the island on the *Scaffie*, the same boat I sailed as a boy and the same boat you just heard so much about. Truth be told, he did all the sailing as I lay on my back in the bow, looking up at the red sail and the blue sky, delighting in the gift of being a passenger.

We didn't talk much, as is normal for us in moments like that. We used only the words we needed, sparingly, like fresh water on a long ocean passage. After a dozen tacks back and forth, beating our way into the wind, we reached the shallows of the north end of the island. I dropped the sail, and he pulled out the oars to row us into the shore. I wore my rubber sea boots and stepped off onto the gravely rocks, keeping my feet warm and dry. He kicked off his Vans and jumped ashore with bare feet before sprinting up the rocks and into the woods.

We met a little while later at the other end of the island, on the bluff by the lighthouse where the view stretched to the horizon. There we stood in the blinding sun reflecting off the ocean. The Graves jutted from sea, just a dark silhouette far to the south, the last hard stop between here and Matinicus, an island twenty miles offshore. Beyond that lay Africa.

I was grateful to have him here—in the full meaning of "here"— though I did not want to embarrass him or make the moment awkward with paternal sentimentality. But, since we were both looking in the same direction, and since we were both safe and warm, and because three years had passed since that cold call in California, I took the chance to ask him my question one more time.

"So where do you think you were when you left the boat?"

We looked over the water together, squinting, for the light was too much to take in unguarded.

"A little beyond half-way between here and The Graves," he said.

My vision suddenly got blurry with too much water in my eyes, but I could see clearly that he was telling the truth. I still don't believe it. But it was true.

The boundless gratitude in that blinding light was not without shadows that stung. The old question that arrived when I was a ten-year-old boy was still with me. For I know parents who have lost children. I have held them in their rage, praying to God that I would have the strength just to hold them as they struggled to take another breath in the worst moments of their lives. Their sobs—the dreadful sound of which I have only heard from throats of grieving parents when a wave of truth emerged that was too wrong to believe. The very sound of such grief sounded like, felt like, a condemnation of God. I have been the priest who led those parents to the pew in church and said the funeral words in when no words were a salve for the pain. Their child was loved—is loved—every bit as as my breathing son. This tender awareness cautions me to be careful—terribly, tenderly, awfully careful, with how I dare to share my gratitude for this thing that happened. The ocean of tears, I know, is unfathomably deep.

Whatever lessons or insights my son learned from his marine incident that day are for him—and hopefully, someday, his children. What I learned from that day is beyond my ability to easily explain. Too many words get in the way. Suffice it to say that it forced me to accept that my skepticism kept me from believing something that was obviously true. The world of my awareness, described by the walls of reasonable expectations, was preposterously too small. Miracle stories help us to see that if we let them.

I know at times in my life that the fullness of the Easter story lay beyond belief for me. Like fake spring, I did not trust it. But as I stood with Tristan, gazing into the light on the water, I had to accept that the goodness came together here was more than I could know. I allowed myself to hold gently that Easter is kind of like that.

My Easter sermon, by the way, was short. I did not share everything I just shared here. I stayed out of the way of the story, but I told the truth. And it was good news.

(This essay comes from the larger work Reflections of a Boatyard Priest.*)*

Emma at Home, 2020, by Amy Wilton

Have You Met My Daughter?
Wendy Dyer

As I stood atop Cadillac Mountain in Acadia National Park on Earth Day in April of 1990, I felt as if I had finally found my way home after a lifetime of wondering who I was and where I came from. Citizens of the four tribal nations of Maine had gathered for a sunrise ceremony on Acadia's highest peak. It's a sacred spot to the masses, but particularly to the People of the Dawn. In the darkness, before first light, standing there on the summit, I began to weep.

My tears were of relief and gratitude that my search to find my biological parents had ended. I was filled with emotion finally knowing that I was a citizen of the Passamaquoddy Nation, newly found information that explained so much about my personality and sense of being. I had spent my first twenty-five years feeling different from my adoptive family, peers and neighbors. I often felt like an outsider growing up, like I didn't belong. In those moments on Cadillac prior to sunrise, as I listened to the drums and songs of my ancestors, I felt connected to the earth and to other human beings in a way that I had never experienced before.

It had been almost a year since I had called my birth father, Wayne Newell, a well-respected Passamaquoddy leader and forward thinker who had devoted his life trying to preserve the language of his ancestors and to improve the quality of life of those within the tribe. Legally blind since birth, he was a man of vision. He was known throughout the state and country for helping bridge the gap of understanding between the Native and non-native worlds.

When I phoned him that day, I asked if he knew my mother back in 1964. He said that he did but after I asked if he might be my father, he quickly replied, "No, oh no, it's not possible. That's just not possible." Out of frustration and disappointment, I hung up the phone without telling him my name. I had taken a risk to call. His denial pierced my heart like the sting of a wasp.

My first reaction was to hang up but instead of giving up, I wrote a letter to him with my name and intentions, then asked him to search his soul. When he received my letter a few days later he immediately called. After we had previously talked, he realized that he was likely my father and had been frantic for several days not knowing my name or how to find me.

We agreed to have blood work done to be certain. Paternity tests confirmed our shared DNA three months later and thus began my journey to come to know myself as a Passamaquoddy woman. Finding my birth family was a lot to process, but even more so when I found out that I was of mixed race, and that I had been purposely disconnected from my cultural heritage and teachings.

It was upsetting to know that racial indifference was why I was ripped from my white mother's arms, withheld from my Native father's knowledge and kidnapped from my tribe and culture all because of the color of my father and my skin. I felt a great deal of negativity toward my birth mother's father who had declared that he wanted nothing to do with a Passamaquoddy baby. He sent my birth mother away so that no one would know she was carrying the child of a man from the neighboring reservation. He was embarrassed and disgusted.

The mentality in child welfare at that time was to adopt out as many Native children to non-native families as possible to give the children what was perceived as a "better" life with more opportunities. My adoption was before the Indian Child Welfare Act became law. Had I been born after 1978, an effort would have been made by child welfare to connect me with my father or to place me within the tribe.

Finding my way back was the easy part, finding acceptance for what had been stolen from me took many years to achieve. In the early days, the culture was foreign to me. I didn't know the language, customs or teachings. I had grown up with the whitewashed, textbook, Hollywood version of our country's history filled with inaccurate information, unmerited generalizations and stereotypes. I had not been taught about the tribal nations of Maine. I didn't know there were three reservations within two and a half hours from the island where I was raised. There was so much that I didn't know.

As the sun rose over Acadia that day, it was the first time that I heard drumming. I was mesmerized. Though it was my first experience, it seemed as if I had always heard the drum. I didn't know the words but the songs were so familiar. My father's voice rose above the others that morning as he sang and prayed. I was uncertain what I should do, so I awkwardly followed the cues of those gathered when we turned to face the four directions as they prayed in our Native tongue. We smudged with sage. They sang, danced and drummed.

Over time, I learned the songs, how to drum and dance. I've smudged and prayed on many occasions. I went into sweat lodges, accompanied tribal members on memorial canoe trips, climbed our sacred mountains and took part in many different ceremonies. Each time I did something new it took great courage. Many times I was hesitant but reminded myself that those things were my birthright, so I stretched myself in ways I had not thought possible.

For the next thirty plus years, I accompanied my father to similar gatherings where he shared a part of himself to help the world better understand Native People and our history. My favorite memory was when I accompanied him to Washington DC, to watch him perform at the Library of Congress then at the Kennedy Center. It was truly one of the best days of my life, a memory that sustains me and one that I will forever cherish.

Just before Christmas in 2021, I stood over my father's hospital bed in his living room on the reservation. The last words that he said to me were, "Have you met my daughter?" It was a line that he always used to introduce me to his friends and acquaintances at the events we attended together. Though we had been separated for twenty-five years, we shared a special bond over the next thirty-one. I was humbled that he carried me in his heart even as he lay dying. As he drew his last breath, I had a deep sense of gratitude that I had found him and my tribe, and for the relationship that we had shared. He touched my life in countless ways. He was a father to me in every sense of the word.

Learning the Passamaquoddy teachings and traditions has taken a great deal of effort and dedication. Doing so has given me many profound and moving experiences. My greatest heartache has been that I was disconnected from the language of my ancestors that had been passed down for thousands of years. Though my siblings understand the Passamaquoddy language, I have only learned a few words and phrases. So many of our cultural teachings are held within the language. I cannot pass those teachings on to my offspring in our Native tongue.

It is often difficult to go beyond what is comfortable but doing so brings a feeling of empowerment. I have learned so much but still have so much more to learn. I marvel at the resilience of the Passamaquoddy people. We have somehow overcome all of the attempts to wipe us off the face of the earth. Our cultural teachings, language and customs have endured one attack after another but we have survived. Many, like me, were taken from our culture but somehow we found our way home. We as a People are still here. I am still here. Had I not stretched myself many times along the way, I would not have known my father or found my place within my tribe or be the person that I am today. I would have missed out on some of my life's most precious and finest moments.

Roofing the Woodshed
Leslie Moore

My husband works above. I'm grounded.
He straddles rafters, bracing a work boot on one,
knee on another, reaching into his carpenter's belt
for the nail set to punch holes through the metal.
The blows of his hammer echo across Smith Cove.

Five o'clock in the morning, still cool,
clear light. A hermit thrush pipes plaintive
scales in the woods as my husband fits special screws
into his gun, zips them through the metal,
snugs them into the purlins.

I steady the ladder, hold each metal sheet
in place until the first screw catches it, snag
the wayward hammer that careens down a trough,
find the expensive screws that spin
into the blueberry patch behind the shed.

My husband is too old to be up there clambering
over wet rafters. That's why I'm here.
I swat mosquitoes, feel the dew soak through
my shoes, listen to the zip, zip, zip of the screw gun,
and tether him to safety with my presence.

Widowmaker
Leslie Moore

A storm snaps the poplar fifteen feet up.
Its upper story catches in the sugar maple's
embrace, where it broods over our house.

A *widowmaker*, Tom calls it, dangerous to leave
hanging, dangerous to take down. He consults Bruce,
the neighbor. Together they pace around the tree,

peer into snaggled branches, ponder height,
fall line, kick back. They retreat to their garages.
Return armed with tools.

Tom hasn't wielded a chainsaw
in six years. He's eighty. I worry.
They circle the tree again.

Tom lassos the leaner, rigs the line
to a snatch block, ties the block to a tree.
Bruce yanks the starter cord of his chainsaw.

His wife peers out their window, as Bruce
uses his ten-foot extender to saw wedges
from both sides of the splintered trunk.

The poplar shifts on its pedestal.
More circling. More discussion. They give
a mighty tug on the line. Nothing.

Tom ties the line to Bruce's pickup, orders
me and the dog out of range. The line stretches.
Stiffens.   Twists.   Thins.

The butt end kicks off and the tree topples
with a great whoosh and a lordly thud,
taking a litter of broken boughs with it.

It falls between our house and my studio,
just shy of the deck. No longer a menace.
No widows today.

Houses in the Lakes Region I
Jefferson Navicky

Bunny says she knows how to find a good parlor to park herself in. She is highly metaphysical and her sleeves are tearing from wear. Bunny has a simple song to play for you about what went wrong, because there's nothing more critical than the little ol' rumor hole. Bunny chases her luck and her cats and it's a delicate thing she does to maintain her household of fur and largesse. Bunny has a heart the size of a honking wood stove. Lordy. You should see the size of that thing. The cats swarm her with a look of HelloMommaWeLoveYou. Bunny knows how to make a killer stew and knows where her whole cumin seeds lead her.

In a former life, Bunny imagines she was a Maine Coon who parked himself in front of the wood stove and didn't move unless fed giblets. For her current incarnation, she is a small gray cat who often chooses to not go outside, because of many reasons, but mainly because she would just rather not. Bunny grew up among wolves and her first best friend was her last. Walking down a country road in the middle of the night, Bunny thinks about what she left back there, way back. And Bunny went through her phases that she sometimes spells "fazes" because she was too dazed by moonlight to change her mind. She has a good nook. Many of them. And gardens. And a barn where the rafters tower over her barn cat who she named Froggy. The rest of the cats have names too, but names are not always important. Bunny let go of some urban stuff to move out here to the outskirts of the town named after a European city. That was a trend in the 19th century—name the country town after a cosmopolitan hub—Paris, Brooklyn or even after an entire country where a bunch of her relatives were from: Norway. Bunny likes this old house she rambles through. People say, "That's a lot of house" and the phrase sounds like she's in a buffet line and finds herself inadvertently grabbing an especially large, but delicious pork loin. The house gives back to her in its number of fireplaces, and the central hallway big enough to set up an extra bed. Bunny goes to bed early. The sky up on the ridge looks like it might sit on her shoulder like a cat.

Houses in the Lakes Region II
Jefferson Navicky

I was born standing in front of that window looking out on the lilac tree. My childhood was leaves. I hit my teenage years with Tilly the giant orange tabby in the old barn with the squeaky boards where if you weren't careful you could step on one end and find yourself catapulted into another dimension. I wasn't ready for that. I tried to be careful with my watershed body, but it had a mind of its own. I met a man who wanted to cover me in the equivalent of vinyl siding—for your own good! he said. Fat chance—luckily Bunny raised me to know my mind and to spot a shyster. I took a job on the ridge, and spent most of my time in the cold rain and I was happy until I met a woman who said, it's time to uphold our responsibility to the past. I didn't really know what she was talking about, but I liked the way the light hung off her hair, so we went into it together. I found myself the Tallest Man on Earth, which turned out to be incredibly fortunate because our old farm house always seemed to need a section of the roof replaced and I got good with the hammer of my hands. And the best thing, looking back, I never once felt the burden of tomorrow. It was the past that sustained me.

The Cleaving of a House
Jefferson Navicky

They carved the house in two so that it could be moved three miles away into the country. The house had sat on Main Street in the old coastal New England town once known as the destination for huge trees that would become the masts of whaling ships. The house had to be moved to make way for the McDonald's made to look like an old colonial house from the outside, but on the inside, it looked just like a McDonald's. The old house was put together piece by piece, reassembled, then sold to a young couple buying their first house. The man was a carpenter and said of the way they put the old house back together again: "it's not the way I'd have done it…" The young couple put a huge wood stove into the house, bigger than the recommended size, but still the house was often cold and drafty like its heart had been broken in two, and no method of stitching could truly unite it. Houses don't like change, but the young couple did their best to bring the house back to health. Back in the old coastal New England town that no longer looked very much like an old New England town, the McDonald's on Main Street was breaking all regional sales records.

Joe on the Moosehead Railway Line, 2021, by Amy Wilton

Milliken's General Store
Judy Kaber

(after Berenice Abbott's 1954 photograph of the same name)

From the front porch of Ralph M. Milliken's store, men sprawl,
throats dry in the sun & dust edged day. One man in front looks away,
wants the visible world doused, the woman with camera gone.

From my back steps crabgrass, a spread of sand. The whole world
a toxic playground. Any of them could have been my father, any of them
could have shredded hearts and lined the world with chicken wire.

Signs: *Clothing—Shoes—Groceries—Feed*. As if this is all you'll need, as if
all the promises haven't been hollowed out with spoons, as if a lung
hasn't been scooped away. As if *Salada Tea* answers dreams.

After I left home, left the page of what I was supposed to be, my breath
filled with cinnamon, the weave of moments like blind pennies in my mouth.
          Flickering scenes out bus windows.
In the photograph one man smokes,

hair iron-gray, legs spread, boots rooted. In their mouths, taste of salt,
          black soil, the way the
dirt spins up from the plow. Now only this sitting, this inverse of waiting,
          these same stories,
wads of tobacco, intermittent choke and cough.

Night of the Bear
Judy Kaber

Not full night, but twilight. Someone came
and told us about it. A neighbor, I guess,
who else would it be? A shot bear lay
heaving in the bushes at the base
of our driveway. I was in a cotton nightshirt
with a wool sweater over it, hammock
of heat from the wood stove
wrapped around me. I went and stood
at the crest of the drive, arms crossed,

watching the knot
of men that hovered around the shrubs,
not wanting to go in, to hurry
what might turn out to be the jolt
of the bear rising again. This was before
everyone carried a phone in his pocket.
We didn't even have one in the house.
Otherwise I suppose
someone would have called
the game warden, but no one did.

Late summer or early fall, trees still
clinging to spasms of leaves. Little
traffic on the road. No hunter here
on the hill or in the valley below. Only
the crash and clash of the bear

into the edge of woods.
Something made me want to break
the sun's low contentment,
leave dishes unwashed on the table,
traipse out in slippers, past the rusted-out engine,
the pile of bricks from the old chimney,

and glimpse the soft shadow
of the bear's back. To see if it moved
with his breath or only from the nudge
of excited boots, young men
who still had so much to do in their lives, who
weren't afraid to get on their knees
beside a dead bear, while I stood too far away
to see the wet muzzle, to understand dominion.

Notes from the Country
Tonia Denico

I can almost hear Esmeralda Chicken's voice this morning, muttering and clucking in quiet and only semi-disgruntled approval at the cool mild morning. My poor hen hated molting and when it started would rage pluck herself naked overnight in sheer fury just to get it over with, then stalk through the yard cold and furious with life until she became beautiful again.

This fall, with its gentle mist-rising mornings and warm days would have made her so happy. The fog today fell heavy from the trees. It was a bare regret away from rain and the black etched branches had to struggle against it to be seen in the morning light. Her small, determined body would have already been busy in the leaf piles, chiding me for being late.

This month, where green finishes its journey to red, gold, and orange before drifting to the ground.

This month, with hot crackling blue days and pale cool amber afternoons.

This month, when the moon sits so clear and sharp in the sky you could almost cut yourself on the cold white light.

This month, with morning fogs that drape the world in haunts.

This month, with great jagged strings of geese crying across the dusk.

This month, gives and takes of light and dark, before and after, ending but beginning. You can't get to Spring again without resting in the dark.

There was a small rain tonight, barely enough to dampen the tired ground. More than enough to grow a sliding warm fog over the field that smells of far-away places and screams of loud cricket voices. Are there more crickets in a fog or does the sound just echo in that drifting wall of gray. I'm watching it creep down the hill, waiting for it to cross the grass and slip through the window. Waiting for it to bring me the smells of jungle and wild that only a ghosty summer fog can hold.

There is a tiny valley behind my house. It's filled with tall straight trees, stillness, and, when there is enough water, a small brook. I came here tonight looking for some quiet but found instead small birds discussing bugs, seeds, and appropriate bedtimes. I found the small brook bubbling and muttering as it hurried around green fuzzy rocks and the tall stretching trees whispered to the breeze. I sat and listened to all this business and let the long sun slide up the valley and dance over me, turning me a little gold to match the light on the water.

For whatever reason, this day made me long to be outside, to connect with something more real than the elusive problems of the world. So, I walked. And remembered. Chasing snakes out of the juniper bushes, the small ponds at the edge of the cow pasture, the rickety barn where it was fun to climb hay bales, the cresting whaleback of ledge that was the best place to play. All spots long gone. So much gone, changed, lost, like bits of me drifted away and I felt disconnected . . . until I noticed the light.

The same light has leaned on this rock wall, on me, on these trees every golden afternoon. Even when I didn't notice. It will lean on us forever, holding us together, making it all real at the edge of the afternoon.

The wind that ripped and tore at the morning left the day cold but so beautiful. The sun tonight pours like thin gold through the small valley behind my house and has set the owls calling and calling. It's still chill enough to make my fingers sting, but the light is whispering of warmth and last season's brown grass smells sweet and toasted and green underneath. Spring is moving in on the light, creeping up from below, promising more.

Sometimes it seems as though memory is not just a thing of the mind but of the fingertips and of smell. Of hearing and taste and that pinch at the edge of your heart. I remember so many things this way. The dusty thump of horses' hooves on the little path under the willow. The willow that saved all its slippery hissing leaves and twisty finger branches for the fall lawn—never the pasture. A bother to rake, forcing you to stop and clean the rake constantly, but perhaps that was so you would also stop and look at the day, the sky, the graceful tree.

There is a feel to spring lamb fleece. Tight and bumpy as a hooked rug, all soft folds on tender skin and ears fat and warm. Tails thrashing with joy as they nurse from bottles almost pulled from your hands in demand and after, milky chins that need rubbing and love.

The sharp clean bitterness of wood cured in a dry rock-walled cellar. A smell that sits on the back of your tongue as you choose the longest burning log. Muscle in your lower back pinched tight front stooping low or maybe from just waiting for that imagined spider to finally fall. Bits and pieces, images stuck in all the places memory can hide. The corner of your eye, the tip of your fingers, the edge of your heart

On the small hill behind my house the snow has whispered into fog, leaving the ground bare and brown. Brown is such a simple color and yet it makes me restless for the feel of dirt on my fingers, for the rich simple sun-warmed smell of life. I want to lust over baby tomatoes and touch their leaves and dream of heated drowsy summer.

That tiny patch of brown will most likely disappear again under spring snow at least once but it has done its job. My heart already blooms toward a new season.

There are small slices of light now at each end of my day. Small slices where I can see some pale gold, where the trees show their grace, and the barn is less dim. Small bits of light I can gather inside myself for when I have to turn away from my life, go to work, smile too hard, pretend to laugh; give, give, give, until there is nothing left but shadow.

But I can hold that light, drive home in its thin cool glow, and see the peach bloom of the sunset. I can hold on, even when the cold is a blue misery in my joints, because the sun is getting stronger. And I am holding light.

There is no blue sky or warmish breeze. The air is full of ice and bitterness, but my discomfort with myself and my four walls needs to be pulled apart by cold and green, so here I am. Each breath is sharp, painful. It tastes of the cold memory of winter and makes any color left bold and fierce. It's a hard walk to come back from, this winter forest that pulls you so far out of yourself that as you leave you have to stop, gather your edges in, fold them back from where they have journeyed among the trees and small valleys. Put yourself together to step into the world again.

The edge of the sun this morning lifted the night, leaving a clear blue light to shine in the woods. There were no shadows in this barely light, even though the moon stayed, caught in the branches a whisper past full. The only sound was my body shushing through the small snow. Just me, this cold, blue-lifted dawn, and the tiny broken stillness. All finding calm.

The mist last night was unseasonable as it crept and rolled across the fields and between the naked trees. It left a flavor on my tongue like February thaw. Was it any wonder I saw such wild things in the pale and ghosty light. It would not have surprised me to hear the mad laughter of Spring Heeled Jack or the hiss and creak of a great silver dirigible as it raced to hide in the clouds. What else do you expect this close to a full moon, when the mist tastes of metal and wild phantom light?

The moon is full tonight. Round and glowing and glorious but also cold. So cold. Tonight, it is the color of bone and pain and the clouds dragged across its face bear too much resemblance to regret.

Deep fall is the time of year that calls you to walk in the woods one more time while the earth is still giving under your feet. To breath in the deep smoke of fallen leaves and the mossy breath of trees. To watch the small brooks run with fingers of ice at their edges and feel the first deep chill creeping up from under the dark evergreen places.

To walk in the woods on a morning when the sky is the color of a ripe peach, so you can see fall laid bare and know that the dark may come but also go. The peaches will ripen in the orchard. There will be heat and heavy light and children's laughter flung like banners across the sky.

So stand in the forest, breathe in the cool green and dream, and dare to eat peaches in the summer and let the juice run down your breast.

Walking down the road after work and chores tonight, it wasn't late but the light had mostly bled from the sky. The plum dark remains of light were just enough to show the black grace of tree crowns branching into the sky.

The small wind drifting up the field brushed my lips and eyes with a cold that matched the falling dark. This is the dark I brace myself against.

Every year at season change, as the light fades more, I dig deeper for the fire and heat of other seasons, other places, other times. Warmth and light that burn inside are not always easy to find, but worth the hunt. And good to share.

The caterpillar ate and watched the sky. Watched the clouds, the birds, the dizzy translucent butterflies and felt the lifting breeze and yearned, but there were things to do first. Always things to do. A house to build. A whole shape to change. A new thing to become. But something was wrong and there would be no flying, one part wasn't perfect, the gossamer torn.

So, this new life that should have drifted and soared learned small joys in walking and tended just one small space of blooms. Not the wide world of a whole field. But those blooms were special.

And then suddenly it was over, and everything was dusted with icy lace. The small clinging feet that had only walked let go . . . and were lifted by the breeze that had strength enough, and those feet danced with the leaves at the end of the season and flew so very far and wide.

Where you are is beautiful but don't forget it's never too late to fly.

Lavender

Ellen Taylor

It's Voting Day at the Appleton village fire station, where we dutifully
file
in like obedient house cats, follow the red arrows that point to ballot
stations,
then past orange cones that signal danger, past racks of firefighting jackets
with neon yellow stripes, yellow hats, tall rubber boots and thick gloves,
through the office/kitchen/rest area with donated electric stove, crooked
fridge, tired blue plaid couch with filling spilling out. Here is where
you'll find the library bake sale, a biannual event, with hermit bars,
double fudge brownies—well-labeled to warn of nut dangers—beside
a plate of Penelope's cheesy scones, Eliza's blueberry muffins, a loaf
of banana bread, chocolate chip cookies, Snickerdoodles.
Donations welcome, accepted, expected really.

All voters must pass here to exit, past the waft of chocolate raspberry
Bundt cake and oatmeal molasses cookies: Men with John Deere hats,
men with suspenders, with the blue shirts of car mechanics, with bow ties
and suit jackets; Women too, with designer quilted purses, with hemp
bags,
with platform shoes, with no shoes but flip flops. Women in skirts, in
Carhartt's,
in yoga pants and in pant suits; Voters with tee shirts from the Common
Ground
Fair, with *Dump Trump*, with *FJB,* with *Down with Mills, Vote
LePage* Ts.
All stop by here, to exit the building.

Donations welcome, for the library, the non-partisan building across the
      street,
with a Welcome Sign, with a free book table, with fiction and nonfiction,
      with poetry,
Maine authors, with books on democracy and books on tyranny.
      Donations
welcome. Women have been baking all week, sifting and mixing,
      spooning and
scraping batter into muffin tins and pans, their kitchens topsy turvy with
      floured
counters and bowls in the sink, eggshells in the compost and sugar dusting
      the floor.
If your diet won't allow those sweet consumables, a local farm has donated
four lavender plants. Lavender, known for its soothing scent, its delicate
purple buds peeking above spiked leaves bent skyward. Lavender: from
      the Latin
Lavandula, to wash. Good for aches and tension, for post-natal pain and
      hot flashes.
Lavender, for your bathroom soap dish, your pillow, your sock drawers.
      Lavender:
for your tea, your sachets, for your pleasure to rub between your fingers.
A democratic plant everyone agrees on: Lavender,
      for the library, for all.

Festival Nocturne, by Jim Nickelson

Seeing the Stars at Night in Maine
Sarah Walker Caron

In childhood, I would gaze at the dark blue night sky draped over my New York home searching for the bright moon, sometimes but a splinter in the sky. If I was lucky, a few stars would be there too and I'd rattle off a childhood rhyme to make a wish when I spotted one.

Above my head, there was curiosity. Back then, the Earth still felt like the center of the world—a big, important place in the universe.

But when I moved to Maine, I discovered how small we are in the vast universe. And it happened because one night I simply looked up.

That first time, I was startled to see the dark sky spread with a patchwork of pinpricks—some clustered in a milky array, others twinkling brightly on their own. A totally different sky spread above us — one that was so vast, so unexpected, so overwhelming. As I took it all in, realizing that I could stare up and never see everything above us, I was humbled.

Famed cosmologist Stephen Hawking, who spent decades researching and theorizing about the universe, encouraged curiosity. I thought I knew that curiosity before coming to Maine but it was limited by what I knew of the sky.

"Look up at the stars and not down at your feet. Try to make sense of what you see, and wonder about what makes the universe exist. Be curious," Hawking said.

Where I grew up, my friends and I would lay outside and search for the Big Dipper and its companion the Little Dipper. We'd try to pick out the North Star too. And, if we were lucky, we'd see a star shooting across the sky. This happened on beaches and sleepaway camps. Sometimes it happened in our backyards. If we saw a dozen stars, it was a magical night. That sky we saw was vast enough to spark our imaginations about what may be out there.

Looking up at the night sky here in Maine, you can feel how small we are in the immensity of the universe. It takes my breath away. I could spend days searching for adequate words for this and still not quite capture the vast, expanding marvel that is our universe.

Fortunately, Maine's stunning nighttime sky is not going unnoticed.

In 2021, the land in the 100-Mile Wilderness between Moosehead Lake and Baxter State Park, owned by the Appalachian Mountain Club, became the first International Dark Sky Park in New England, meaning it's one of the darkest stretches of sky left in this region. The lack of light pollution allows us to gaze at enormously starry nights and see so much more of the world beyond our planet.

These days, when my kids and I head south to travel and visit family, I see the sky differently. I notice how bright the night sky is in southern New England. I see how few stars we can find there. And I realize what a tiny window there is for us to see anything approaching true darkness there.

It's easy to focus on the world we see—the things we're doing, the people we spend time with, whatever's happening around us—and lose sight of the bigger picture. Here in Maine, when you look up on a clear night, you can see that we are one planet in a universe of millions.

"Who are we? We find that we live on an insignificant planet of a humdrum star lost in a galaxy tucked away in some forgotten corner of a universe in which there are far more galaxies than people," astronomer Carl Sagan said.

And that's exactly it.

Pink Cadillac
Charlotte Crowder

"Just heard on the scanner, some lady from Massachusetts followed her GPS onto the old dump road got her car stuck in the junk yard," Edith said.

"'Magine that." Henry shut the back door behind him.

"Road's been closed for years. All brambles. Quite a feat to drive a vehicle all the way up to the junk yard."

Henry nodded and stooped to take off his work boots.

"Goes to show what happens when folks depend on those new-fangled things. Why, if she'd used a map, she would have known there was no road there. Billy up to the fire house said he's not willing to use his volunteers to get her out of the fix. I just put supper on the stove, but we should go haul her out before dark. We can take the four-wheeler. It'll handle the terrain. Put your boots on."

"Just took 'em off."

Henry trudged across the dooryard and hoisted himself onto the John Deere. Edith swung her leg up and over behind him and wrapped her arms around his girth. The four-wheeler rattled down the dirt road, kicking up dust and pebbles. Henry turned in at the thicket that marked what had once been the dump road. He plowed through the brambles, thorns catching at their clothes, and on up the hill into the woods. A mile and half up they reached the junk yard. Old refrigerators with their doors torn off and covered in moss leaned against busted-up cars and rusted propane tanks sunk deep into the peat moss.

"Why it's a Caddy," Edith said as they approached the car caught up in a tangle of bed springs. "And a pink one at that."

"Remarkable."

"And, my word, doesn't her hair match?"

A tiny woman sat on the hood of the car, swatting blackflies. Her hair was not colored in an old-lady pink rinse, but dyed a shocking magenta. Her legs hung over the car's hood. Tufts of lichen were caught on her spike heels. She wore a black pencil skirt and pink bolero jacket.

Edith waved her arms as the four-wheeler mounted the last crest of the hill. "Helloo," she called.

"Oh, I am so relieved to see you," the pink lady called back. She leapt from the hood of the car, driving her spike heels deep into the moss.

Henry stopped the four-wheeler next to the Cadillac and Edith jumped off to help the pink lady extract herself from the moss. "Now just how did you get yourself into this mess?"

"It's my first trip in this car. See I'm the Mary Kay lady."

"Nice to meet you, Mary Kay."

"No, no, I'm the Mary Kay lady. I sold the most product nationally this year and earned the car. I had this idea to expand my territory. Come up to Maine where ladies don't use much make-up. Seemed to have market potential. But the GPS led me astray."

"Well, never mind that now. You're coming home to supper. You must be starved."

"Certainly am. Been stuck here since before lunch."

"It's hen clams and dilly beans tonight."

The pink lady wrinkled her nose.

"Hop aboard, dear."

"But what about my car? My brand new car?"

"Will have to leave it for now, dear. You come on home with us, and we'll settle all this in the morning."

"Why, I couldn't impose."

"Nonsense, you're in a fix. You'll stay with us."

"Well, I guess I'll need my night things. And I'd like to show you my products. I think you could use a good blusher and some lipstick. I've got all the latest colors. Trouble is, I'm not sure I know how to open the trunk."

"Henry here is an automobile mechanic. He can figure that out."

Henry lumbered over to the car, clicked the catch on the trunk, and returned with two small pink leatherette suitcases, which he handed to the pink lady. He climbed on to the four-wheeler.

"Hop aboard," said Edith. "In that tight skirt, looks like you might have to sit side-saddle. I'll take your bags."

The three jounced down through the thicket—Henry bent over the steering wheel, the pick lady hanging desperately to the seat, and Edith with one leatherette suitcase in each hand.

Edith had turned the stove back on and spooned supper on to plates. The kitchen smelled of vinegar from the dilly beans. "Hen clams are pretty tough," Edith commented as she watched the pink lady push the food around on her plate, "I admit, they do take some getting used to."

"Oh no, they are perfectly delicious."

"The guest bed is up in the loft," Edith said, "You'll have to climb the ladder. If I were you, I'd take off those ridiculous shoes before doing so."

The pink lady nodded. She tried a small forkful of clams and wrinkled her nose. Henry passed his plate for seconds.

As they all folded their napkins and pushed their chairs from the table, the pink lady announced, "Now I will help with the dishes and then, Edith, I would like to show you my products. And perhaps we could plan a Mary Kay party for tomorrow and you could invite some friends and neighbors over to see the products."

With the table cleared, the pink lady opened one of the leatherette suitcases and spread out her wares—mascara wands; pots of blusher; jars of foundation; tubes of lipstick in a range of reds, oranges, and pinks; and eye shadow in tiny translucent containers, which revealed shades of pale lavender to darkest plum. She propped a mirror in the middle of the table, then lined up a series of bottles of various creams—wrinkle removal cream, night cream, day cream, cream to remove age spots.

Henry cast a skeptical look at the table and retreated to the den with the large screen TV.

"I've never fussed with such stuff," Edith said.

"That's fine. Just let me show you what make-up can do for you. Now just sit right down in this kitchen chair."

Edith acquiesced and the pink lady got to work, starting with the creams. "Now these creams don't work right away. They take time, three weeks to a month, to remove wrinkles and liver spots. You just have to use them every day, morning and night. Then you'll see a difference."

Edith was as skeptical as Henry, but sat patiently as the pink lady applied the creams and then a foundation.

"This foundation has a slight rose tone, which matches your skin color. Brings out some highlights in your auburn hair, too."

Edith reached up to pat her hair. "Thank you for saying so, dear, but my hair's mostly gray by now."

"Add a bit of blush for a healthy glow, and to emphasize those high cheekbones of yours. And eye make-up."

Edith smiled at herself in the mirror.

"And mascara, nothing too dark—sable brown, perhaps—will show that you really do have long eyelashes. With a bit of eye liner, your eyes will be prominent. Then, all you need is lipstick. Lipstick lifts the face. I happen to have a special on Peach Sunset this week. I think it's the perfect color for you, very subtle."

"Why, I don't know myself," Edith said, looking into the mirror again.

"You look wonderful."

"But I feel like my skin can't breathe. Like it's all clogged."

"Oh, you'll surely get used to that."

Edith walked into the den, stood in front of the wide-screen TV. "Henry, what do you think?"

"Don't know what to think," he said.

"Henry says it'll be past noon before they can get the tow truck up to the dump road to pull out your car," Edith told the pink lady at breakfast the next morning.

"Why that's just perfect. There will be time for a Mary Kay party."

"Well, I guess so. If any of the girls have the time."

"Oh, please try and see."

Reluctant, Edith began calling. "Have a houseguest, Mary Kay. She has these beauty products she wants to show. If you have time, come about 10:00. I'll have coffee and fresh-made doughnuts."

The girls were curious; they made time. Dorothy didn't drive anymore, so she came with Millicent. Coming through the door, they presented an odd contrast. Dorothy was tiny and stooped, with rosy cheeks and a head of tight gray curls. Millicent, straight-backed and tall had stark white hair that hung in a thick braid down her back. Annie completed the trio. She was big-boned with skin leathered from sun, her hair close-cropped, salt and pepper. She came straight from the garden, dirt under her fingernails and ground in to the knees of her overalls. She had walked from her house down the road and arrived slightly out of breath.

The pink lady had again set up the cosmetics on the kitchen table. Edith's doughnuts, fragrant and still warm, sat on the kitchen counter next to the coffee pot and an array of mismatched mugs.

Edith did the introductions, "This here, is Mary Kay."

"Actually, my name is . . ."

Edith continued, "She wants to show you her products."

The pink lady sat the girls down in turn and did a full make-up job for each one, expounding the qualities of the products as she worked. Dorothy went first. She lowered herself into a chair and listened intently as the pink lady explained that wrinkles would begin to disappear in just three weeks. Every few minutes while the pink lady worked, Dorothy looked over at the mirror and nodded with approval at her reflection.

With a flourish of the blusher brush, the pink lady pronounced Dorothy done. Dorothy smiled again at her reflection in the mirror. "And, Peach Sunset lipstick is on special. It's the perfect color for your complexion."

"Why Dorothy," Millicent said, "you'll charm the pants off your beau at the Grange Hall. Did you girls know that Dorothy has a beau?"

"Nonsense," Dorothy said. "Clyde's just a dance partner. The Grange Hall has a dance every Saturday night. He lives with his mother. Has for seventy-seven years. Last week, he told me he's a virgin."

"Dorothy, think what you could teach him!" Annie said as she settled into the chair and succumbed to the pink lady's ministrations. The pink lady massaged several different creams into Annie's leathery skin, then picked a foundation in a deep tone. After outlining Annie's eyelids in a deep brown she announced, "To finish, what you need is Peach Sunset lipstick."

As Millicent sat down in the chair, Annie began to scratch her cheeks.

"Why, Annie, you are all bumps," Edith said. Pink hives erupted all over Annie's face.

"Never you mind," said the pink lady. "I have a cream for that." She dug through one of her leatherette cases and produced a bottle of cream, which she applied over Annie's foundation. "This will take several hours to work. But those hives will go soon. Don't you worry."

Millicent looked sceptical. "I'll have none of that," she said as she watched the pink lady unscrew the top of a bottle of wrinkle removal cream. "At my age, you're supposed to have wrinkles. And believe you me, I've earned every one of these."

The pink lady hesitated and reached for a bottle of foundation.

"Don't want that either," Millicent said. "Prefer my natural pallor."

The pink lady did not give up. "You have such luminous blue eyes. We'll pick a shade of eye shadow to offset them. Eye shadow, mascara, and a bit of eye liner and they will really pop."

Millicent sat straighter in the chair, pulling back her shoulders and assented to this final suggestion.

Made up, Millicent and Edith looked uncomfortable with their new images. Edith held her face taut, as if afraid the foundation would crack. All four wore Peach Sunset lipstick. Dorothy was still smiling. "I wonder what Clyde will think of the new me," she said, and the others shared covert smiles.

There was a pink quilted draw-string bag filled with samples for each of them. Scratching at her forehead, Annie politely declined the offer. Her lips had puffed up and her eyelids were beginning to swell. She looked like a prize fighter who had wandered into a poison ivy patch.

The tow truck, pulling the pink Cadillac rumbled into the driveway. Festoons of lichen and brambles hung from the undercarriage. There were a few scratches running the length of the car. While Henry worked with the truck's driver to lower the car to the ground, Edith bustled around in the den, and the pink lady packed up her supplies. The group moved to the driveway to see her off. Annie took one of the leatherette suitcases and Millicent carried the other. Edith held a Maine road atlas.

"Now Mary Kay," Edith said, "see that you use a proper map to get yourself back to Massachusetts. This here is the *Maine Gazetteer*," she said, waving the road atlas. "Couldn't get around the state without this. Why, we have a copy in each of the vehicles and a few extra in the house. This one's for you."

"Why thank you. How thoughtful of you, Edith." the pink lady climbed into the front seat, hampered by her pencil skirt. She took some time adjusting her seat back and the sideview mirrors. With a determined thrust of her index finger, she pushed the button of her GPS to switch it off, then eased out of the driveway as everyone waved good-bye.

Edith turned to go back inside, "Can't wait to wash my face."

Dirt Road Christmas
Tim Sample

I was in my mid-twenties, just married, and living in a one-room cabin with a wood stove and an outhouse on a dirt road in Palmyra, Maine. Jimmy Carter was president. Home mortgage rates were hovering around 20% and gas prices had recently doubled. I figured it was the perfect moment to embark upon a full-time career in the arts.

I did okay at first. All summer we got by on what I earned singing "Horse with No Name" in local bars and hand lettering actual names on pulp trucks.

Our nearest neighbors were the Spragues—Forester Sprague, universally known as "Fod," his wife Mary, and their sons, a hardscrabble farm family for whom "gettin' by" was a way of life. About two miles in the other direction was a makeshift commune of young back-to-the-landers from exotic faraway places like Pennsylvania.

As autumn approached, these hipsters packed up their incense, love beads, and wind chimes, climbed into an old school bus, and headed for sunnier climes. Before embarking however, they stopped by to inform us that their erstwhile pet hog Francis Bacon would be spending the winter in the Spragues' chest freezer. If we wanted ham, pork chops, perhaps a pound or two of Francis's actual bacon, we need only drop by and ask. Just ask. No problem, I thought and made a mental note.

Winter came early and hit hard that year. By late November the ground was frozen solid as granite. Finding work was even harder than that.

For the first time in my life, I found myself worrying whether we'd have enough food to eat. With Christmas just around the corner, cheer was in short supply.

Then, on a dark December afternoon, it dawned on me. Just a mile up the road there was a freezer full of pork chops, bacon, and maybe even a roast waiting to be transformed into a holiday feast. All I had to do was ask. Is that so difficult? Well, it sure seemed like it to a young man determined to make his own way in the world. Necessity, however, is a great motivator and I soon found myself trudging up the icy road to my neighbors' farm.

Of course, it wouldn't be a short visit. Rural Maine etiquette in a situation like this calls for coffee, a few games of cribbage, and random speculation on topics like the Red Sox and deer hunting. I did just that for an hour and a half, knowing that eventually I'd have to ask "the question." When I finally got my nerve up, Fod's uncharacteristically sharp response startled me.

"You want some of that meat do ya?" he said, fixing me with a withering glare. Then, turning abruptly he called to his wife Mary in the next room and together they clomped noisily down the cellar stairs, returning a few minutes later with several large grocery bags overflowing, not just with the frozen meat I'd asked for, but a month's worth of home grown, home canned beets, corn, tomatoes, relishes and jams, potatoes, and similar staples.

Fod warmed up his truck, we loaded in the groceries, and he drove me home. Even with the heater blasting, the atmosphere inside the cab was chillier than it was outdoors. After we'd unloaded all the bags, I turned to say goodnight. Fod gave me another hard look, crooked his finger in a "come over here" gesture and I walked over and stood face to face with him in the snowy dooryard.

Suddenly, he raised his hand, wagged a finger at me and hissed, "Don't you ever do that again!" I was stunned. Embarrassed doesn't even begin to cover it. Despite the frigid air, I could feel my face burning with shame. "Don't you," he continued, "ever, *ever,* **ever** sit down the road from me and be hungry again! I simply won't have it!" For a long moment his words seemed to hang in mid-air and then they gradually began to sink in.

He continued, explaining that he and Mary had spent countless hours each fall preparing and canning fruits and vegetables and "putting up" various other foods for the coming winter. They'd done this as long as he could remember. As a result, he told me, "We've got good food down cellar we're gonna have to pitch out cause it's been there so long!"

As he said it his whole face exploded into a marvelously warm, wrinkly, gap-toothed grin. Reaching out his hand, he grasped mine, gave it a hearty shake, and said, "Merry Christmas, Tim!"

It turned out to be exactly that.

Contributors

Ellen Baker is the author of the novels *Keeping the House* and *I Gave My Heart to Know This* and the forthcoming *The Hidden Life of Cecily Larson*. She lives in Round Pond.

Selected by President Obama as the fifth Presidential Inaugural Poet in U.S. history, **Richard Blanco** was the youngest, the first Latinx, immigrant, and gay person to serve in that role. In 2023, Blanco was awarded the National Humanities Medal by President Biden from the National Endowment for the Humanities. Blanco has received numerous awards, including the Agnes Starrett Poetry Prize, the PEN American Beyond Margins Award, the Patterson Prize, and a Lambda Prize for memoir. Currently, he serves as Education Ambassador for The Academy of American Poets and is an Associate Professor at Florida International University. In April 2022, Blanco was appointed the first-ever Poet Laureateof Miami-Dade County.

Laura Bonazzoli's fiction has appeared in numerous publications, including *Evening Street Review, Exposition Review*, and many others. "Fish, Birds, Light" is from her collection of linked short stories, *Consecration Pond*. Laura has also published personal essays and poetry in more than thirty literary magazines and several anthologies.

John Paul Caponigro is an internationally collected visual artist and published author. He leads unique adventures in the wildest places on earth to help participants creatively make deeper connections with nature and themselves.

Sarah Walker Caron is a journalist, food writer and the author of eight books, mostly on food and cooking. Her writing has appeared in *Bangor Metro*, The *Bangor Daily News*, *Paste Magazine*, *The Girlfriend*, *Bella Magazine,* and others. She's a Barnard grad, a mother of two and a firm believer in the healing power of the ocean.

Charlotte Crowder lives and writes on the coast of Maine. She is a medical writer and editor by day. Her publications include, among others, stories in *Tamarind Magazine, Present Tense, Intima, Branching Out: International Tales of Brilliant Flash Fiction, American Writers Review*, and a picture book, *A Fine Orange Bucket.*

Tonia Denico is a healthcare professional and homesteader living in Central Maine.

Wendy Dyer is a citizen of the Passamaquoddy Nation, and a graduate of the University of Maine at Machias. Her story "A Warrior's Homecoming" appeared in *Dawnland Voices: An Anthology of Indigenous Writers from New England.* Several of her stories have been published in the online literary magazine *Dawnland Voices 2.0*, two *Chicken Soup for the Soul* books and in *Homeschooling Today* magazine. She was one of the winners of the 2022 Maine Writers & Publishers Alliance Call for Native Writers, and is a 2022 Ashley Bryan Fellow. She works for Wayfinder Schools.

Becca Shaw Glaser's writing is published in *The Rumpus*, *Women's Studies Quarterly*, *The Columbia Journal*, *Entropy*, *The Offing*, and *Mad in America*. Co-editor of the book, *Mindful Occupation: Rising Up Without Burning Out*, she was an editor at *The Maine Commons*, a grassroots Maine-based paper, and *Salt Hill*. She has an MFA in poetry from Syracuse University and lives in midcoast Maine.

Chrystena Hahn holds a B.A. in English and an M.A. in Writing. She made a career editing textbooks, teaching high school and college

English, and supervising literacy from pre-K through high school. In 2019, Hahn relocated to Maine to make a life in which she might become a working poet. Maine has provided the breathing room she needed.

Alexandra Hinrichs is a poet and award-winning author of children's fiction and nonfiction picture books, including *The Pocket Book, The Lobster Lady,* and *I Am Made of Mountains.* She lives in Bangor, Maine.

Judy Kaber is the Poet Laureate of Belfast, Maine, and author of threechapbooks, most recently *A Pandemic Alphabet.* Her poems have appeared in journals such as *Poet Lore, december, Hunger Mountain Review,* and *Spillway.* She won the 2021 Maine Poetry Contest and was a finalist for a 2022 Maine Literary Award.

Jeffrey Lewis is a professional captain, educator, and an ordained Episcopal Priest. After starting his career as a naval officer, he spent many years in character and spiritual education of young people, first at the Hurricane Island Outward Bound School and then as chaplain and teacher at high schools in New England. He currently captains an old wooden schooner and serves as vicar of the Union Church on Vinalhaven island. He and his wife, Susan, have been married for thirty years and three sons in their 20s, all of whom currently live in Maine. His forthcoming book, *Reflections of a Boatyard Priest* is expected to come out in 2024.

Christine Terp Madsen recently returned to Maine after a hiatus in other parts of the country. She can still feel the thrill that she got the first time she crossed the Piscataqua River into Maine some fifty years ago. She was immediately caught up in the landscape, the wildlife, and the culture. She is a retired editor, but keeps on writing—a novel and a memoir sit unpublished in her desk, but her poetry has seen publication in a dozen or so journals.

Shawne McCord began life on the Pacific coast and settled in Maine not far from the Atlantic coast, living full years of love, learning, poetic pursuits, capturing wonders with photography, as well as teaching and parenting with perseverance. She was awarded the Academy of American Poets undergraduate prize while studying poetry and photography. Writing, in many forms, has been a steady ingredient in her life and career as an educator.

Born and raised on Mount Desert Island, **Audrey Minutolo-Le** teaches writing and literature at the University of Maine. She is the author of poetry, plays, essays, and travel literature. Her non-fiction work has been published by Down East Books, *Down East Magazine*, and *Habitat: Magazine of the Maine Audubon Society*. Her poetry has been published with The Poet's Corner, and her plays have been presented at The Women's College in Sydney, Australia and the May Sinclair Society at the University of Sheffield, England. She divides her time between the coast of Maine and California, two landscapes that inspire and challenge her creative spirit. Her first novel, *Gray Ledges,* will be published in 2025.

Hazel Mitchell is originally from England where she attended art college, now she lives in Swanville, Maine, where she has her studio. As well as creating fine art and photography Mitchell is a children's author and illustrator. Her work has received several awards and been recognized nationally. She has exhibited both in fine art and illustration exhibits.

Leslie Moore is a poet and printmaker whose subject is often animals. She is the author of *What Rough Beasts: Poems/Prints* and winner of the 2018 Maine Literary Award for Short Nonfiction. She has published poems and essays in *English Journal, Take Heart, The Maine Review, The Catch, Café Review, Balancing Act 2, Deep Water, ArtWord 2021, Wait: Poems from the Pandemic, 3rd Wednesday, Kerning,* and *Tellus Journal*

(Italy). Her art may be found in book illustrations, private collections, and at the Local Color Gallery in Belfast, Maine.

Jefferson Navicky is the author of four books, most recently the novel-in-prose-poems, *Head of Island Beautification for the Rural Outlands*, as well as *Antique Densities: Modern Parables & Other Experiments in Short Prose*, which won the 2022 Maine Literary Book Award for Poetry. He is the archivist for the Maine Women Writers Collection.

Based in Camden, Maine, **Jim Nickelson** works as a fine art photographer, custom digital printer, bookmaker, and teacher. Before committing himself to the photographic life, he was a NASA engineer and corporate attorney. Jim has received numerous awards, including being honored as Artist-in-Residence at Acadia National Park, Chiricahua National Monument in Arizona, and the Baer Art Center in Iceland. He was also honored as Book Artist-in-Residence at Maine Media Workshops + College.

Tim Sample is a Maine native whose unique New England style of humor has gained him a national following. Legendary newsman Charles Kuralt has called Sample "Maine's Humorist Laureate." Tim has written and/or illustrated over a dozen books, including regional bestsellers *Saturday Night at Moody's Diner* and *How to Talk Yankee*. Tim's narration work includes such award-winning films and audiobooks as Robert McCloskey's children's classic *Burt Dow Deep Water Man* and Stephen King's *The Sun Dog*

Pam Burr Smith has published short stories, essays, articles, and poems in many journals, including, Georgia Review, Kansas Quarterly, Slow Dancer, and Cafe Review. She has published three volumes of poetry, Heaven Jumping Woman, Near Stars, and Speaks, and a book on narrative therapy, Living Conversations. She was awarded an Honorable Mention by Mary Oliver in the 1994 MWPA Poetry

Chapbook Contest. In 2021, she won the Finest Poem Prize at the Plunkett Poetry Festival. After a career as a therapist, she is returning to painting. She has been writing poetry all her life, and lives in Brunswick, Maine.

Ellen M. Taylor is a professor of English at the University of Maine at Augusta, where she coordinates language and literature, and regularly teaches in the prison education program. She organizes the annual Plunkett Maine Poetry Festival, held each April in Augusta. She is the author of three collections of poetry, *Floating*, *Compass Rose*, and *Homelands*.

Susan Tenney is an Award-winning director/choreographer as well as a poet. Her work in theater has been seen in venues that include Lincoln Center, Cincinnati Playhouse, La Mama, McCarter Theatre, and Williamstown Theater Festival. She is the recipient of four commissions from the Princeton Coalition for Peace Action to create The Hiroshima Commemoratives, and by the Princeton Council for the Arts to create the multi-disciplinary work, The Tower, performed in five languages. Her poetry has been published in the Ekphrastic Review and in the book Remember: A Tribute to Veterans and Their Families.

Phoebe Walsh grew up in Camden, Maine and is a student at Smith College. She hopes to combine her studies at Smith College with her background in woodworking to ultimately push the boundaries of what defines furniture. She also explores all sorts of artistic mediums, including photography and printmaking.

Meg Weston's poems have appeared in *Hawaii Pacific Review, Trouvaille Review, Red Fez, One Art, Writing the Land, Goose River Anthology*, and her books, *Letters from the White Queen* and *Magma Intrusions*.

Amy Wilton is a multimedia artist best known for her powerful photographic portraits that appear to engage the sitter in creative conversation. Amy's mixed media artwork is broad in its use of various media, from oil on board to found object sculptures and installations. Amy has been featured at Cove Street Arts in Portland and shown at Fotonostrum in Barcelona for the Barcelona Biennial. She holds a BFA in Photography from The George Washington University and an MFA in Photography from Maine Media College.

Lucinda Ziesing is a writer, actor, painter, and producer. She received an MFA in writing from Spalding University. As a mixed media artist, her Public Works paintings are in private and corporate collections. She also taught on the Theatre Faculty of Sarah Lawrence College and has appeared in classic and original productions in New York, Los Angeles, and Maine. When she is not writing, she produces outdoor events that bring wonder to the communities of Maine.